FROM "INTER INSIGNIORES"
TO "ORDINATIO SACERDOTALIS"

CONGREGATION FOR THE DOCTRINE OF THE FAITH

FROM "INTER INSIGNIORES" TO "ORDINATIO SACERDOTALIS"

Documents and Commentaries

PREFACE
MOST REV. TARCISIO BERTONE

INTRODUCTION
CARDINAL JOSEPH RATZINGER

COMMENTARIES
H. U. VON BALTHASAR, J. L. BERNARDIN, I. BIFFI,
J. BURGGRAF, J. CORBON, A. DESCAMPS, J. LITTLE,
G. MARTELET, A. G. MARTIMORT, J. RATZINGER,
R. SPIAZZI, M. THURIAN, A. VANHOYE

UNITED STATES CATHOLIC CONFERENCE
Washington, D.C.

Translations of the Vatican documents and commentaries: *L'Osservatore Romano,* English edition.

Cover photo courtesy of the archives of the Studium Biblicum Franciscanum, Jerusalem.

First Printing, March 1998

ISBN 1-57455-163-X

CONTENTS

CONGREGATION FOR THE DOCTRINE OF THE FAITH DECLARATION "INTER INSIGNIORES" REGARDING THE QUESTION OF THE ADMISSION OF WOMEN TO MINISTERIAL PRIESTHOOD

COMMENTARIES

JOHN PAUL II
APOSTOLIC LETTER "ORDINATIO SACERDOTALIS"
ON RESERVING PRIESTLY ORDINATION
TO MEN ALONE

FOREWORD TO THE ENGLISH EDITION

This book is a translation of volume 6 of the Congregation for the Doctrine of the Faith's series *Documenti e Studi*. It contains the text of the CDF's declaration *Inter Insigniores* of 1976, Pope John Paul II's Apostolic Letter *Ordinatio Sacerdotalis* of 1994, and the CDF's reply to a *dubium* concerning the teaching contained in the Apostolic Letter (1995). In addition, the book offers commentaries on these documents that appeared in *L'Osservatore Romano* in 1977, 1993, and 1995. It constitutes a sort of handbook for the study of the Church's most recent teaching about who is able to receive the sacrament of holy orders.

One of the things that becomes clearer in the study of these documents and commentaries is that one cannot understand the import of an answer if one has not grasped what the question is. The discussion about "women's ordination" is not really about power in the Church or the equality of the sexes. It is about the nature of the sacraments and the extent to which the Church is free to deal with them. The teaching of *Inter Insigniores* and *Ordinatio Sacerdotalis* is that the Church is simply not able to confer priestly ordination on women because it has not been authorized by Christ to do so and that this is not a matter of church law or discipline but of Christ's determination. The issue to which these documents speak, therefore, is the issue of Christ's lordship over the Church.

The NCCB Committee on Doctrine is happy to present this translation of authoritative documents and commentaries about holy orders, and it hopes that their publication in English will assist in the understanding and assimilation both of the answers that have been given and of the questions that are addressed in this issue.

✠ Daniel E. Pilarczyk
Chairman
NCCB Committee on Doctrine

PREFACE

The present volume differs from the others in this series which are all dedicated to single documents.[1] It presents the text of the declaration *Inter Insigniores* on the question of the admission of women to the ministerial priesthood, which was published by the Congregation for the Doctrine of the Faith on October 15, 1976, with the approval and at the direction of Pope Paul VI. It also includes the text of the apostolic letter *Ordinatio Sacerdotalis* on reserving priestly ordination solely to men, promulgated by Pope John Paul II on May 22, 1994, as well as the *"Responsum ad dubium* concerning the teaching contained in the apostolic letter *Ordinatio Sacerdotalis,"* published by the same congregation on October 28, 1995, with the approval and at the direction of Pope John Paul II.

The unity of this volume arises from the argument or question of the non-admission of women to priestly ordination. It was deemed helpful and necessary to include not only the declaration *Inter Insigniores,* with its respective commentary, but also to provide readers with the more recent statements of the magisterium: the apostolic letter *Ordinatio Sacerdotalis* and the subsequent *Responsum ad dubium.* In these later documents, the question has been revisited in order to give definitive clarification regarding the doctrinal character of the Church's practice in this area and the kind of assent which is owed to this teaching.

The volume contains, in chronological order, these documents of the magisterium together with their respective commentaries and explanations.

The book begins with an introduction by His Eminence Joseph Cardinal Ratzinger, Prefect of the Congregation for the Doctrine of the Faith. This introduction is essentially the text of the cardinal's

---

[1] This English book is a translation of volume 6 of the Italian series *Documenti e Studi.*

authoritative commentary on the apostolic letter *Ordinatio Sacerdotalis*, which was published in English by *L'Osservatore Romano* on June 8, 1994. It illustrates the organic connection between this papal document and the declaration *Inter Insigniores* and explains the fundamental reasoning and ecclesial significance of the teaching of these two documents. The authority of *Ordinatio Sacerdotalis* and the relative kind of assent which its teaching requires from the faithful are explained. Finally, the principal ramifications of the teaching are noted, with respect to contemporary questions of culture and anthropology, and in the area of ecumenism. The cardinal's original article has also been revised to include references to the *Responsum ad dubium* which, as mentioned above, was published subsequently.

The declaration *Inter Insigniores* is presented next, accompanied by a commentary prepared at the request of the Congregation for the Doctrine of the Faith and published in *L'Osservatore Romano* at the same time as the declaration. This is followed by a series of articles by respected authors such as R. Spiazzi, H. U. von Balthasar, A. G. Martimort, G. Martelet, J. Bernardin, and J. Ratzinger, which were printed in *L'Osservatore Romano* in the months following the promulgation of the declaration and which explore in greater depth individual aspects of the question.

Another series of articles on the teaching of the declaration *Inter Insigniores* is also included; these were published in *L'Osservatore Romano* in the spring of 1993 in the context of the debate, which took place also within the Catholic world, over the decision of the General Synod of the Church of England to ordain women. These articles illustrate the biblical foundation of the Church's teaching in this area (A. Vanhoye), the witness of tradition and the theological reasons for the teaching (I. Biffi), the ecumenical implications of the question of the nature of the priesthood, whether in the dialogue with Christians of the Reformed tradition (M. Thurian) or with the Orthodox Churches (J. Corbon). Finally, the question is considered in the context of the promotion of women in the life and mission of the Church (J. Burggraf) and in the perspective of the feminist debate (J. Little).

Lastly, the volume presents the apostolic letter *Ordinatio Sacerdotalis* (1994) with the *Note of Presentation* that was published at the same time in *L'Osservatore Romano*. These are followed by the *Responsum ad dubium* (1995) concerning the teaching contained in the apostolic letter, together with a commentary provided by the Congregation for the Doctrine of the Faith and published in *L'Osservatore Romano*.

This volume, which is characterized by density and compactness, will undoubtedly prove to be of great benefit, especially at this historical juncture, for those who not only wish to know the doctrine of the Catholic faith on a topic which touches upon the divine constitution of the Church, but who also rightfully demonstrate the need and the desire to deepen their understanding of the doctrinal principles and theological reasoning. In this way, the question of ministerial priesthood will be removed from misleading claims and incorrect and confused methodological approaches. The perspective of authentic Christian anthropology, so often recalled and highlighted by Pope John Paul II in his encyclical letters and discourses, will be strengthened, as the proper context for the promotion and rediscovery of the mission and essential role of women in evangelization and in the life of the Church.

✠ Tarcisio Bertone
Secretary

INTRODUCTION

1. The Reason for the Document and Its Context

In the apostolic letter *Ordinatio Sacerdotalis,* on reserving priestly ordination to men alone, the Supreme Pontiff Pope John Paul II has not proclaimed a new doctrine. He is simply confirming what the whole Church—East and West—has always known and lived in faith. She has always recognized in the figure of the twelve apostles the norm of all priestly ministry and has submitted to this norm from the outset. For her part she knew that the twelve men, with whom according to the faith of the Church priestly ministry has its origin in the Church of Jesus Christ, are bound to the mystery of the incarnation and are thereby appointed to represent Christ—to be, as it were, living and acting icons of the Lord.

In this century two factors have caused the previously undisputed certitude concerning the will of Christ in instituting the Church to appear to many as more and more questionable. Where Scripture is read independently of the living Tradition, in a purely historical way, the concept of institution becomes less evident. The origin of the priesthood is then no longer seen in the nascent Church's recognition and acceptance of the will of Christ, but in a historical process not preceded by any clear founding will, and which therefore could have developed in a fundamentally different way. In this understanding, the criterion of institution for all practical purposes loses its validity and can therefore be replaced by the criterion of functionality. This development of a new relation to history combines with the anthropological upheavals of our day. The symbolic transparency of the corporeality of man, which is self-evident to a sacramental way of thinking, is replaced by the functional equivalence of the sexes. What was previously the bond to the mystery of origin is but now regarded as discrimination against half of humanity, as the archaic holdover of an outdated image of man that must be opposed by the struggle for equal rights. In a world thoroughly characterized by functionality, it has become difficult even to conceive of viewpoints other than those of functionality. The real nature of the sacrament, which is not derived from functionality, can hardly be perceived at all.

Given this situation, it was the duty of the papal magisterium to recall the essential contents of Tradition. In the same context is to be found the declaration of the Congregation for the Doctrine of the Faith *Inter Insigniores,* on the question of the admission of women to the ministerial priesthood, published on 15 October 1976 with the approval and at the direction of Pope Paul VI.

The declaration's central affirmation is the following: "The Church, in fidelity to the example of the Lord, does not consider herself authorized to admit women to priestly ordination" (*Inter Insigniores,* Introduction). With this statement, the magisterium professes the primacy of obedience and the limits of ecclesial authority. The Church and her magisterium do not have an authority coming from themselves, but only from the Lord. The believing Church reads and lives the Scripture not in the form of historical reconstruction, but within the living community of the People of God of every age. She knows herself to be bound to a will which precedes her, to what the Lord instituted. This will which precedes her, the will of Christ, is expressed for her in the choice of the Twelve.

The new document, signed by the pope himself, builds on the declaration *Inter Insigniores* of 1976 and presupposes it. At the same time, it stands in continuity with other subsequent texts of the magisterium which touch on the same theme in larger contexts:

• In the apostolic letter *Mulieris Dignitatem,* the Holy Father writes: "In calling only men as his Apostles, Christ acted in a completely free and sovereign manner" (no. 26).

• In the post-synodal apostolic exhortation *Christifideles Laici,* the pope declares: "In her participation in the life and mission of the Church, a woman cannot receive the sacrament of Orders, and therefore cannot fulfill the functions proper to the ministerial priesthood. This is a practice that the Church has always found in the expressed will of Christ totally free and sovereign, who called only men to be his Apostles" (no. 51).

• The *Catechism of the Catholic Church* again takes up the same doctrine, affirming that "the Lord Jesus chose men (*viri*) to form the college of the Twelve Apostles, and the Apostles did the same when they chose collaborators to succeed them in their ministry. . . . The Church recognizes herself to be bound by this choice made by the Lord himself. For this reason the ordination of women is not possible" (no. 1577).

2. The Basic Statement of the Text

Despite these clear affirmations of the magisterium, the uncertainties, doubts, and disputes about the question of the ordination of women have continued also in the Catholic Church and become in part even more intensified. A one-sided understanding of infallibility as the only binding form of decision in the Church has become a lever for relativizing the documents mentioned above and for thus asserting that the question is still open. This state of uncertainty on a question touching the core of the life of the Church obliged the pope to intervene anew, for the explicit purpose "that all doubt may be removed regarding a matter of great importance" *(Ordinatio Sacerdotalis*, no. 4).

If the Church openly and unambiguously expresses here the limits of her authority, this surely has practical consequences in the realm of discipline, but it is not all just a disciplinary question, that is, a problem of ecclesial practice. Rather, the practice is the expression and concrete form of a doctrine of faith. Priesthood, according to the Catholic faith, is a sacrament, that is, not something invented by the Church for pragmatic reasons but something given to her by the Lord. Consequently, she cannot give it any shape she wishes; instead she can only hand on in respectful fidelity what she has received. The question of the subject, that is, of the possible recipient of ordination, is already given and is not subject to the Church's decisions. It is a question pertaining to the Church's constitution itself *(Ordinatio Sacerdotalis,* no. 4).

The apostolic letter distinguishes two levels of the Church's doctrinal statements on this point:

a. The doctrinal foundation of the teaching and practice of the Church is found in the example of Christ, expressed in the choice of the Twelve, who then received the title "Twelve Apostles." This institution of Christ, which followed a night spent in prayer with the Father (cf. Lk 6:12, 16), is described in the document in its theological depth from Scripture: Jesus' choice is at the same time a gift from the Father. Accordingly, the testimony of Scripture has been understood and lived from the beginning and without a break in Tradition as the binding commission of Christ. The magisterium knows itself to have been placed in the service of this interpretation.[1]

b. If then the will of Christ, as attested to by Scripture, lived in Tradition, and interpreted by the magisterium, is the essential reason for the Church's teaching, it is not enough to view this will positivistically as a kind of arbitrary norm. Christ's will is always a

---

[1] Again and again, the normative meaning due to the institution of the group of the Twelve is relativized. The materially rich contribution of W. Beinert is impressive ("Dogmatische Überlegungen zum Thema Priestertum der Frau" in ThQ 173 [1993]: 186-204). A detailed discussion of the arguments he proposes would go beyond the scope of this brief essay. But even without great discussions it should be apparent that Beinert's examples of non-normative actions of Jesus cannot be put in parallel with the choice of the Twelve. "Although Jesus . . . was philanthropic, he still did not free the servant of the centurion of Capharnaum from slavery" (p. 189). The omission of a socio-revolutionary action can hardly be placed on the same level as the positive act of calling the Twelve, which proceeds in the New Testament from the heart of the messianic consciousness of Jesus (cf. the Bible text in no. 2 of the document). The same is true *mutatis mutandis* for the following example: although Jesus "emphasized the value of celibacy for the sake of the kingdom of heaven, he nonetheless called the married man Peter to be the leader of his flock . . ." (p. 189). Also the further examples given on p. 191 for the directions and forms of behavior of Jesus forgone in the further development do not take into account, on the one hand, the specific character of the calling of the Twelve, and on the other, the specific literary form and historical classification of the texts in discussion (the ban on oath-taking; the ban on preaching to the pagans—before the cross and resurrection!; participation in the Jewish cult and separation therefrom—in the year 70 the cult as such was extinguished!).

will of the *Logos,* that is to say, a will full of meaning. The task of the believer seeking to understand the faith is to look for the meaningful in this will, so that it can be communicated and lived according to its meaning and with interior acceptance.

In fact, the above-mentioned declaration *Inter Insigniores* in its fifth section devotes itself at length to the attempt to understand interiorly the will of Christ. In contrast, the new document limits itself essentially to the first level, without ignoring the importance of the second. The pope places a limit on himself here. He recognizes his duty to emphasize the fundamental decision which the Church does not have the power to make for herself but must accept in fidelity. He leaves to theology the task of drawing out the anthropological implications of this decision and of showing its soundness in the context of the present-day dispute about man. What I indicated at the outset about the symbolic-sacramental vs. functional views of man shows how difficult such a task is. But it also shows how necessary and rewarding it is to devote oneself to it. To be sure, the Church has something to learn from the modern view of man, but the modern world too has for its own part something to learn from the wisdom which is preserved in the tradition of faith and which cannot be dismissed simply by labeling it archaic patriarchalism. Where namely the connection is lost to the will of the Creator and, in the Church, to the will of the Redeemer, functionality easily becomes manipulation. The new esteem for woman which was the justified point of departure of modern movements ends then soon in contempt for the body. Sexuality comes no longer to be seen as an essential expression of human corporeality, but as something external, secondary, and ultimately meaningless. The body no longer reaches what is essential to being human, but comes to be considered an instrument we employ.

But let us return to the self-imposed limitation of our document which, as has been said, regards anthropological reflections not its task but one for theologians and philosophers. With this limitation, the pope once more clearly places himself in the basic line of discussion initiated by *Inter Insigniores.* The point of departure is the bond to the will of Christ. The pope becomes thus the guarantor of obedience. The Church does not herself invent what she should do, but discovers in listening to the Lord what she must do and let stand. This viewpoint was critical for the decision of conscience of those Anglican bishops and priests who now feel themselves impelled to join the Catholic Church. As they have explained with ample clarity, their decision is not a vote against women but a decision for the limits of the Church's authority. This is clearly articulated, for example, in Bishop Graham Leonard's foreword to the theological history of Anglicanism written by Aidan Nichols. Leonard speaks of four recent developments which undo the structure essential to the dialectic of the Anglican understanding of the Church. The fourth of these developments he sees in "the power which has been given to the General Synod of the Church of England to determine questions of doctrine and morals . . . and to do this by majority votes, as if in these matters the truth could be determined in this way. The Church of England rejects the doctrinal authority of the pope, but the Synod tries to exercise a teaching function which theologically has no foundation and which, for all practical purposes, claims to be infallible."[2] In the meantime similar voices have also been raised in the Lutheran Church in Germany, where for example Professor Reinhold Slenczk strongly opposes the fact that majority decisions taken by ecclesial bodies are practically declared necessary for salvation, and it is forgotten that the "great consensus" in the Church, which the Reformers declared the supreme authority, consists in the agreement of church teaching with Scripture and the Catholic Church.[3] With the new docu-

[2] Aidan Nichols, *The Panther and the Hind: A Theological History of Anglicanism* (Edinburgh, 1993); preface by Bishop Graham Leonard, pp. ix-xiii; citation, p. xii.

[3] R. Slenczka, "Theologischer Widerspruch: Brief vom 16 November 1992 an die EKD," in *Diakrisis* 14 (1993): 187ff. Important p. 188: The *"magnus consensus* which the position appeals to . . . consists, according to the *Confessio Augustana* (CA) I and according to the resolution of Part I of the CA (BSLK 83 c f), in the agreement of ecclesial teaching with Scripture and with the Christian or, as it is called in the Latin text, the catholic Church. It (the *magnus consensus)* is not based on a majority that in the last decades has outvoted or eliminated definitively a minority, but on the truth as the foundation of unity. That we are dealing with the introduction of women's ordination with a novelty in contrast to apostolic teaching and catholic community, even representatives of such resolutions cannot dispute."

ment, the pope does not wish to impose his own opinion but precisely to verify the fact that the Church cannot do whatever she wants and that he, indeed precisely he, cannot do so. Here it is not a question of hierarchy opposed to democracy, but of obedience opposed to autocracy. In matters of faith and the sacraments, as well as in the fundamental issues of morality, the Church cannot do what she wants but becomes Church precisely in assenting to the will of Christ.

3. Methodological Presuppositions and the Authority of the Text

At this point yet another objection may emerge. It may be said: as an idea it is fine and good; but Scripture does not teach it all that clearly. Various passages are then adduced which seem to relativize or nullify this conviction of Tradition. It is pointed out, for example, that in the Letter to the Romans (16:7), Paul supposedly indicates as a distinguished apostle a woman, Junias, together with her husband Andronicus: "They were in Christ before me." The "deaconess" Phoebe was supposedly some kind of community pastor; she is said to have had charge of the community at Cenchreae and to have been very well known also outside it (Rom 16:1-2).[4] In this regard one would naturally first of all have to say that such interpretations are hypothetical and can only claim a very moderate degree of probability. This leads

---

[4] U. Wilckens develops these arguments in conversation with M. Mügge in U. Hahn (ed.), *Der Glaube is keine Privatsache. Gespräche mit Altbischof U. Wilckens* (Hannover, 1993), 147-177, esp. 170f.; cf. also U. Wilckens, *Der Brief an die Römer III* (Benziger—Neukirchen, 1989), 131 and 135f. E. Käsemann evaluates the texts quite differently in *An die Römer* (Tübingen, 1973). Re Phoebe: "The word *Prostátis* used here only in the New Testament cannot according to the context designate the leader or representative of a community. . . . Women . . . appear according to the Revelation of John to have occupied in heretic circles as prophetesses ecclesial positions of leadership" (p. 392). "Andronicus and Junias" are according to Käsemann both male names; he views them to be "Jewish-Christian missionaries," "who . . . may claim the title of apostle . . ." (p. 394). H. Schlier, *Der Römerbrief* (Freiburg, 1977) holds something similar to Käsemann re Phoebe: "*Prostátis* means *per se patrona*, but cannot be understood here in the technical-juridical sense as 'chairman' or 'representative' . . . but generally or metaphorically as someone who extended help and protection to the community and the apostle himself" (p. 441f.). He also sees Junia(s) as a male name; re the title of apostle he says: "The *apóstoloi* who →

us back once again to the question which confronted us at the very beginning: Who is the real interpreter of Scripture? Whence do we gain certitude about what it wishes to say to us? If there is only the purely historical interpretation, and nothing else, then Scripture cannot give us any ultimate certainty at all. The certainty of historical research is by its very nature ever only hypothetical: none of us was there. Scripture can become the foundation of a person's life only when it is entrusted to a living subject—the same subject from which it came itself. It arose within the People of God guided by the Holy Spirit, and this people, this subject, has not ceased to exist. The Second Vatican Council expressed this in the following way: "Thus it comes about that the Church does not draw her certainty about all revealed truths from the holy Scriptures alone. Hence, both Scripture and Tradition must be accepted and honored with equal feelings of devotion and reverence" *(Dei Verbum,* no. 9).

This means that a purely historical certainty—one which prescinds from the faith lived by the Church in history—does not exist. This impossibility of a purely historical basis does not at all lessen the significance of the Bible. The certainty communicated in the teaching by the Church is verifiable in and from the Scripture. Scripture, Tradition, and the magisterium are, according to the Vatican Council, not to be considered as three separate and unrelated things, but rather Scripture read in the light of Tradition and lived in the faith of the Church discloses its full meaning in this living context. The magis-

---

proclaimed the word in pairs as 'companions of the yoke' are either emissaries of a community . . . or traveling proclaimers of the Gospel. . . . From this broad concept of *apóstolos* Paul developed then the concept of apostle, which presumes the 'seeing' of the risen one, and limits it from there then to the 'Twelve' and to himself . . ." (p. 444). J. A. Fitzmyer, *Romans* (Doubleday, 1993) leaves the meaning of the word "diakonos" open here (729f.); re "prostatis" he remarks: ". . . Phoebe was perhaps a superior or at least a leader of the Christian community of Cenchreae. . . . We can only speculate about the kind of assistance she gave . . ." (p. 731). Re Junia(s): "Paul writes *Iounian,* which could be the accusative singular of the female name *Iounía, -as,* 'Junia,' or the accusative singular of the masculine name *Iouniâs, -â,* 'Junias'" (p. 737). To the title of apostle: "The prepositional phrase *en tois apostolois* may mean 'those of mark (numbered) among the apostles' of 'those held in esteem by the apostles'. . . The former sense would mean that Andronicus and Junia were *apostoloi.* This title is not to confuse with *hoi dodeka,* 'the Twelve' . . ." (p. 739).

terium is there to strengthen the interpretation of Scripture made possible by listening to the Tradition in faith.[5]

The Church's Tradition has always recognized in the choosing of the Twelve the act of Jesus which gave rise to the priesthood of the New Testament. It thus sees in the Twelve and in the apostolic ministry of the Twelve the normative origin of the priesthood. Catholic theology too accepts other symbolic dimensions of the group of the Twelve. The latter are also the beginning and symbol of the new Israel. But these additional symbolic dimensions do not detract from or diminish the priestly reality which the Lord established with the calling of the Twelve. For this interpretation of Scripture too the principle mentioned above holds true: "The Church does not draw her certainty about all revealed truths from the holy Scriptures alone."

In view of a magisterial text of the weight of the present apostolic letter, inevitably another question is raised: How binding is this document? It is explicitly stated that what is affirmed here must be definitively held in the Church, and that this question is no longer open to the interplay of differing opinions. Is this therefore an act of dogmatizing? Here one must answer that the pope is not proposing any new dogmatic formula but is confirming a certainty which has been constantly lived and held firm in the Church. In the technical language one should say: Here we have an act of the ordinary magisterium of

---

[5] To the question of what exegetical certainties are possible or unattainable, the article by E. Schüssler-Fiorenza is instructive ("Neutestamentlich-frühchristliches Argument zum Thema Frau und Amt. Eine kritische feministische Reflexion," in ThQ 173 [1993], 173-185). The statement on p. 174 is interesting: "Scholarly studies on the development of Church office are numerous but not conclusive. Their results are dependent on the respective hermeneutic starting point and dogmatic understanding of the Church." The author then depicts from her hermeneutic starting point a picture of development according to which the way from an originally strictly egalitarian community in which "in principle everyone had access to . . . common functions of leadership" (p. 176) is said to lead to an ever stronger patriarchalization whereby severe reproaches are raised against the pastoral letters (pp. 178ff.). The author accordingly sees contradictory positions in the canon of the New Testament itself and in this respect ascertains consistently: "Both, radical equality of everyone and the exclusion of women and others subordinated by Church leadership, can therefore be biblically theologically grounded." In this respect it becomes apparent in this remarkable contribution that whoever demands women's priesthood must dissolve the New Testament canon.

the Supreme Pontiff, an act therefore which is not a solemn definition *ex cathedra*, even though in terms of content a doctrine is presented which is to be considered definitive. In other words, a certainty already existing in the Church, but now questioned by some, is confirmed by the pope's apostolic authority. It has been given a concrete expression, which also puts in a binding form what has always been lived. One might use the example of channeling water from a spring. The water itself remains unchanged but is protected against the possibility of draining away or being lost.

4. Supplementary Questions: Discrimination Against Women? Ecumenical Stumbling Block?

Let us turn finally to two pressing questions of our day: Is this not once again a case of discrimination against women? Does not this hinder the progress of ecumenism?

a) The pope—recalling in this context the declaration *Inter Insigniores*—is concerned about the need, deeply felt today, of eliminating any unjust discrimination against women. On this point, the Holy Father evokes with emphasis the dignity of Mary, Mother of God and Mother of the Church. That Mary, who enjoyed the highest dignity possibly to a creature, did not also receive the specific mission of the apostle and the priestly office clearly shows that the non-calling of women to priestly service in no way is based on a lesser dignity of woman and cannot constitute discrimination against her (cf. *Ordinatio Sacerdotalis*, no. 3).

In order that this statement may become credible, a further clarification about the nature of the priestly ministry is to be sure necessary. In the current discussion on women's ordination, priesthood is understood—and as if this were something self-evident—as "decision-making power." Were this the essence of the priesthood, then it would certainly be difficult to understand why excluding women from "decision-making" and thus from "power" in the Church would not constitute a form of discrimination. We have seen earlier that the specific task of the pope in the Church is to be the guarantor of obedience vis-à-vis the word of God, which is not to be manipulated. The same is true on different levels for bishops and priests. If, for example, in the different councils the priest enjoys the power of veto in questions involving faith and morals, this is not a case of asserting hierarchical privileges against the will of the majority (prescinding altogether from the question of how such majorities are constituted and whom they really represent). It is a question rather of establishing the point where the will of the majority ends and obedience begins—obedience to the truth, which cannot be the product of a ballot. No one who reads the New Testament carefully will find the priest anywhere described as a "decision maker." This way of looking at things can only arise in a purely functional society, one in which everything is determined by us ourselves. In the view of the New Testament, the priest must be understood in the light of Christ crucified, in the light of Christ who washes his disciples' feet, in the light of Christ who preaches, who says: my teaching is not mine (cf. Jn 7:16). Being taken into the sacrament is a renunciation of oneself in order to serve Jesus Christ. Where the priesthood is lived correctly, this becomes clearly visible, and the competing idea dissolves of itself. This is perfectly clear from Polycarp of Smyrna to the Curé of Ars and up to the charismatic priest figures of our own century. The logic of worldly power structures does not suffice to explain the priesthood, which is a sacrament and not a form of social organization. The priesthood cannot be understood according to the criteria of functionality, decision-making power, and expediency, but only on the basis of the christological criterion which gives it its nature as a "sacrament"—as a repudiation of personal power in obedience to Jesus Christ.

To be sure, an examination of conscience cannot be avoided here. Unfortunately, there are not only holy priests but there is also the lived contradiction in which the priesthood does indeed appear to be reduced to decision-making and "power." Herein lies a task of great responsibility for priestly training and for spiritual direction in the priesthood. Where a person's life does not bear witness to the word of faith but distorts it, the message cannot be understood.

In this context, I would like to recall a few words of recent popes which emphasize what has been said so far. As Paul VI put it: "We cannot change what our Lord did, nor his call to women, but we must recognize and promote the role of women in the mission of evangelization and in the life of the Christian community."[6] Pope John Paul II follows this line of presentation when he says: "Above all the acknowledgment in theory of the active and responsible presence of women in the Church must be realized in practice" (*Christifideles Laici,* no. 51).

In explaining the papal document, one must take care to stress the strong recognition of the equal dignity of men and women in the order of sanctity. Everything else in the Church exists only as a support to foster holiness. This is the common goal of all men; what counts finally before God is holiness alone. Together with the equal human dignity of the sexes, however, there is always need to recall their specific missions and thus to resist all new forms of Manicheism, which seeks to reduce the body to something irrelevant, "merely biological," thus depriving sexuality of its human dignity, its specific beauty, and which is only capable of conceiving an abstract and asexual human nature.

b) Finally, a brief word on the ecumenical question. No one can seriously state that this new document represents an obstacle to ecumenical progress. The document expresses the obedience of the Church vis-à-vis the biblical word lived in Tradition; it is precisely a self-limitation of church authority. Thus the document guarantees the unbroken communion with the churches of the East in understanding the word of God as well as in the sacrament which builds up the Church. No new point of controversy in relation to the communities originating from the Reformation is raised, for the question of what the priesthood is, whether a sacrament or finally a service to be regulated by the community itself for its order, has from the beginning been part of the disagreements which led to the division in the

---

[6] Paul VI, Address to the Committee for International Women's Year, 18 April 1975: AAS 67 (1975): 266.

sixteenth century. The fact that the Catholic Church (like the Ortho-dox churches) remains steadfast in her conviction of faith, which she sees as obedience to the Lord, cannot surprise or wound anyone. On the contrary, it will be an occasion for reflecting together even more carefully on the pressing underlying issues: the relationship between Scripture and Tradition, the sacramental structure of the Church her-self, and the sacramental character of the priestly ministry. Clarity in expression and a common will to obey the word of God are the bases for dialogue. No new conflict has been created but rather a renewed challenge to reflect on the existing division from its depths and to seek once more and with ever greater fervor, with eyes fixed on the Lord, the path of unity.

✠ Cardinal Joseph Ratzinger
Prefect

DECLARATIO

CIRCA QUAESTIONEM
ADMISSIONIS MULIERUM
AD SACERDOTIUM MINISTERIALE

VATICAN DECLARATION:
REGARDING THE QUESTION OF THE ADMISSION OF WOMEN TO MINISTERIAL PRIESTHOOD

PROOEMIUM

PARS MULIERIBUS HABENDA
IN NOSTRI TEMPORIS SOCIETATE ET ECCLESIA

Inter insigniores aetatis nostrae notas, Ioannes Papa XXIII, fel. rec., in Encyclicis Litteris suis *Pacem in Terris,* die 11 aprilis anno 1963 datis, eam assignavit *quod ... mulieres in re publica intersunt ..., quod fortasse celerius apud populos fit christianam fidem profitentes, et tardius quidem, sed late, apud Gentes aliarum memoriarum heredes alioque vitae cultu imbutas,*[1] Concilium vero Vaticanum II, in sua Constitutione pastorali, quae a verbis incipit *Gaudium et Spes,* enumerans hos discriminandi modos in iuribus personae fundamentalibus, qui superandi et removendi sunt, utpote Dei proposito contrarii, congruenter primum eum enuntiat, qui a sexu petatur.[2] Aequabilitas vero personarum, quae inde oritur, ad talem hominum societatem aedificandam tendit, quae non sit plane uniformis, sed harmonice componatur et una fiat, dummodo viri ac mulieres suas ipsorum proprias dotes et dynamicam vim in eam conferant, ut nuper exposuit Paulus Papa VI.[3]

In Ecclesiae ipsius vita decursu saeculorum, ut historia testatur, fuerunt mulieres, quae summa efficacitate adlaboraverunt, opera insignia perficientes. Meminisse satis sit earum, quae magnas Familias religiosas fundaverunt, ut sancta Clara Assisiensis, sancta Teresia Abulensis, meminisse eiusdem Teresiae atque Catharinae Senensis, quae scripta posteris tradiderunt tanta doctrina spiritali referta, ut eas Paulus Papa VI albo Ecclesiae doctorum inscripserit. Neque oblivioni dandae sunt innumerabiles illae mulieres, quae seipsas Do-

---

[1] AAS 55 (1963), pp. 267-268.

[2] Cf CONC. OEC. VAT. II, Const. pastoralis *Gaudium et Spes,* 7 decembris 1965, n. 29: AAS 58 (1966), pp. 1048-1049.

[3] Cf. PAULUS PP. VI, *Allocutio ad membra Commissionis a studiis de muneribus mulieris in Societate et in Ecclesia itemque ad Membra Consilii praepositi anno internationali « de muliere » celebrando,* 18 aprilis 1975: AAS 67 (1975), p. 265.

INTRODUCTION

THE ROLE OF WOMEN IN MODERN SOCIETY AND THE CHURCH

Among the characteristics that mark our present age, Pope John XXIII indicated, in his encyclical *Pacem in Terris* of April 11, 1963, "the part that women are now taking in public life.... This is a development that is perhaps of swifter growth among Christian nations, but it is also happening extensively, if more slowly, among nations that are heirs to different traditions and imbued with a different culture."[1]

Along the same lines, the Second Vatican Council, enumerating in its pastoral constitution *Gaudium et Spes* the forms of discrimination touching upon the basic rights of the person which must be overcome and eliminated as being contrary to God's plan, gives first place to discrimination based upon sex.[2] The resulting equality will secure the building up of a world that is not leveled out and uniform but harmonious and unified, if men and women contribute to it their own resources and dynamism, as Pope Paul VI recently stated.[3]

In the life of the Church herself, as history shows us, women have played a decisive role and accomplished tasks of outstanding value. One has only to think of the foundresses of the great religious families, such as St. Clare and St. Teresa of Avila. The latter, moreover, and St. Catherine of Siena have left writings so rich in spiritual doctrine that Pope Paul VI has included them among the doctors of the Church. Nor could one forget the great number of women who have consecrated themselves to the Lord for the exercise of charity or for the missions, and the Chris-

---

[1] *Acta Apostolicae Sedis* 55 (1963), pp. 267-268.

[2] Cf. Second Vatican Council, pastoral constitution *Gaudium et Spes*, 29 (December 7, 1965): *AAS 58* (1966), pp. 1048-1049.

[3] Cf. Pope Paul VI, Address to the members of the Study Commission on the Role of Women in Society and in the Church and to the members of the Committee for International Women's Year, April 18, 1975: *AAS 67* (1975), p. 265.

mino consecraverunt, ut caritatem exercerent vel operi missionali se devoverent, sed nec christianae illae matresfamilias, quae ad suos permagnam vim habuerunt et praecipue in filios fidem transfuderunt.

Temporibus autem nostris, multo maiora vindicantur: *Cum ... nostris diebus mulieres magis magisque partes activas habeant in tota societatis vita, magni momenti est amplior earum participatio etiam in variis campis apostolatus Ecclesiae.*[4] Haec a Concilio Vaticano iussa impulsum excitarunt, qui iam fructus suos edit: quae tamen varia experimenta maturitatem adhuc exspectant. Numerosissimae vero iam sunt hodie, ut etiam Paulus VI dixit,[5] christianae illae communitates, quae apostolica navitate mulierum fruantur; quin etiam quaedam ex illis mulieribus vocantur in partem consiliorum in ambitu tam dioecesano quam paroeciali ad res pastorales investigandas institutorum. Apostolica quoque Sedes iam in quibusdam suae Curiae laboris coetibus partem mulieribus attribuit.

Porro iam ab aliquot annis, quaedam christianae communitates, ex iis quae saeculo decimo sexto vel posterioribus temporibus ab Apostolica Sede Romana separatae sunt, mulieres admiserunt ad pastorale munus non aliter ac viros: quo novo incepto moti harum communitatum sodales vel etiam aliae huiusmodi communitates postulationes et scripta, ut mulieribus latior pateat haec admissio, nunc repetunt, contradicentibus vero aliis. Huius ergo negotii oecumenicum momentum patet, de quo Ecclesia catholica suam mentem aperire debet, eo vel magis quod publicae opiniones late in variis circulis sparsae quaestionem moverunt, num etiam catholica Ecclesia suam disciplinam mutare posset, ut mulieres ad sacerdotalem ordinationem admitteret. Nonnulli immo ex catholicis theologis eandem controversiam aperte agitarunt, pervestigationes incitantes non tantum in sacris Bibliis, in Patrum scriptis, in historia ecclesiastica, sed etiam in evolvendis institutorum et morum historiis, vel in psychologicis et sociologicis scientiis. Ex quo factum est, ut pleraque argumenta, quae conferre possent ad hanc gravem quaestionem solven-

[4] Conc. Oec. Vat. II, Decretum *Apostolicam Actuositatem,* 18 novembris 1965, n. 9: AAS 58 (1966), p. 846.

[5] Cf Paulus PP. VI, *Allocutio ad membra Commissionis a studiis de muneribus mulieris in Societate et in Ecclesia itemque ad Membra Consilii praepositi anno internationali « de muliere » celebrando,* 18 aprilis 1975: AAS 67 (1975), p. 266.

tian wives who have had a profound influence on their families, particularly for the passing on of the faith to their children.

But our age gives rise to increased demands: "Since in our time women have an ever more active share in the whole life of society, it is very important that they participate more widely also in the various sectors of the Church's apostolate."[4] This charge of the Second Vatican Council has already set in motion the whole process of change now taking place: these various experiences of course need to come to maturity.

But as Pope Paul VI also remarked,[5] a very large number of Christian communities are already benefitting from the apostolic commitment of women. Some of these women are called to take part in councils set up for pastoral reflection, at the diocesan or parish level; and the Apostolic See has brought women into some of its working bodies.

For some years now various Christian communities stemming from the sixteenth century Reformation or of later origin have been admitting women to the pastoral office on a par with men. This initiative has led to petitions and writings by members of these communities and similar groups, directed towards making this admission a general thing; it has also led to contrary reactions.

This therefore constitutes an ecumenical problem, and the Catholic Church must make her thinking known on it, all the more because in various sectors of opinion the question has been asked whether she too could not modify her discipline and admit women to priestly ordination.

A number of Catholic theologians have even posed this question publicly, evoking studies not only in the sphere of exegesis, patrology, and church history but also in the field of the history of institutions and customs, of sociology, and of psychology. The various arguments capable of clarifying this important problem have been submitted to a critical examination. As we are dealing with a debate that classical the-

[4] Second Vatican Council, decree *Apostolicam Actuositatem*, 9 (November 18, 1965): *AAS 58* (1966), p. 846.
[5] Cf. Pope Paul VI, Address to the members of the Study Commission on the Role of Women in Society and in the Church and to the members of the Committee for International Women's Year, April 18, 1975: *AAS 67* (1975), p. 266.

dam, acri iudicio expensa sint. Cum vero agatur de tali controversia, quam, saltem uti nunc se offert, traditio scholarum theologicarum vix attigerit, fieri potest, ut in ea nunc evolvenda rationes quaedam necessariae ab iis, qui argumentantur, neglegantur.

Quamobrem Sacra haec Congregatio pro Doctrina Fidei, mandatum exsequens a Beatissimo Patre acceptum eiusque subsequens verba, quae in suis die 30 Novembris anno 1975 datis litteris scripsit,[6] censet nunc resumendum: Ecclesiam, quae Domini exemplo fidelis manere intendit, auctoritatem sibi non agnoscere admittendi mulieres ad sacerdotalem ordinationem; atque aestimat oportere, pro praesentibus adiunctis, ut in luce clariore ponat hanc doctrinam, quae dolenter forsitan a quibusdam percipiatur, unde tamen oriens bonum paulatim discernetur, quippe quae conferre possit ad *respectiva* viri ac mulieris munera altius investiganda.

I. TRADITIO PERPETUO AB ECCLESIA SERVATA

Numquam Ecclesia catholica sensit presbyteralem vel episcopalem ordinationem mulieribus valide conferri posse. Fuerunt quidem primis saeculis nonnullae sectae haereticae, praesertim gnosticae, quae mulieribus sacerdotale ministerium committere aggressae sunt: quod statim Patres animadversum vituperaverunt, utpote quod novum atque in Ecclesia minime accipiendum iudicarent.[7] Sane in eorundem Patrum scriptis haud dissimulanda percipitur contagio praeiudicatarum opinionum circa muliebrem sexum non aequarum, quae tamen fere nihil in eorum pastoralem actuositatem et etiam minus in eorum spiritalem directionem influxerunt. At praetermissis hisce commentationibus, illius temporis ingenio afflante concitatis, aperte legitur, praecipue in monumentis iuris ecclesiastici, quae Antiochena et Aegyptiaca traditio servavit, ob eam propriam praecipue causam

---

[6] Cf AAS 68 (1976), pp. 599-600; cf *ibid.*, pp. 600-601.
[7] S. Irenaeus, *Adv. haereses* 1, 13, 2: PG 7, 580-581; Ed. Harvey, I, 114-122; Tertullianus, *De praescript. haeretic.* 41, 5: CCL 1, p. 221; Firmilianus Caesarien., in S. Cypriani Epist. 75: CSEL 3, pp. 817-818; Origenes, *Fragmenta* in 1 *Cor.* 74, in *Journal of theological studies* 10 (1909), pp. 41-42; S. Epiphanius, *Panarion* 49, 2-3; 78, 23; 79, 2-4; t. 2 GCS 31, pp. 243-244; t. 3, GCS 37, pp. 473, 477-479.

ology scarcely touched upon, the current argumentation runs the risk of neglecting essential elements.

For these reasons, in execution of a mandate received from the Holy Father and echoing the declaration which he himself made in his letter of November 30, 1975,[6] the Sacred Congregation for the Doctrine of the Faith judges it necessary to recall that the Church, in fidelity to the example of the Lord, does not consider herself authorized to admit women to priestly ordination. The sacred congregation deems it opportune at the present juncture to explain this position of the Church. It is a position that will perhaps cause pain but whose positive value will become apparent in the long run, since it can be of help in deepening understanding of the respective roles of men and of women.

I. THE CHURCH'S CONSTANT TRADITION

The Catholic Church has never felt that priestly or episcopal ordination can be validly conferred on women. A few heretical sects in the first centuries, especially Gnostic ones, entrusted the exercise of the priestly ministry to women: this innovation was immediately noted and condemned by the fathers, who considered it as unacceptable in the Church.[7] It is true that in the writings of the fathers one will find the undeniable influence of prejudices unfavorable to women, but nevertheless, it should be noted that these prejudices had hardly any influence on their pastoral activity, and still less on their spiritual direction.

But over and above considerations inspired by the spirit of the times, one finds expressed—especially in the canonical documents of the Antiochian and Egyptian traditions—this essential reason, namely, that by calling only men to the priestly order and ministry in its true sense,

---

[6] Cf. *AAS 68* (1976), pp. 599-600; cf. ibid., pp. 600-601.

[7] St. Irenaeus, *Adversus Haereses,* I, 13, 2: *PG* 7, 580-581, ed. Harvey, I, 114-122; Tertullian, *De Praescrip. Haeretic,* 41, 5: *CCL* 1, p. 221; Firmilian of Caesarea, in St. Cyprian, *Epist.,* 75: *CSEL* 3, pp. 817-818; Origen, *Fragmentam* in I Cor. 74, in *Journal of Theological Studies* 10 (1909), pp. 41-42; St. Epiphanius, *Panarion* 49, 2-3; 78, 23; 79, 2-4: vol. 2, *GCS* 31, pp. 243-244; vol. 3, *GCS* 37, pp. 473, 477- 479.

solos viros ad ordinem ministeriumque vere sacerdotale vocari, quia Ecclesia fideliter servare intendit exemplar illud sacerdotalis ministerii, quod Dominus Iesus Christus voluit quodque Apostoli accurate custodierunt.[8]

Idem animi iudicium aetatis mediae theologos movit,[9] etsi scholastici doctores, cum fidei veritates argumentis ratione conceptis illustrare satagerent, de illa quaestione argumenta saepe hauriebant, quae hodie docti difficile accipiant, immo iure improbent. Ex eo tempore usque ad nostram aetatem non iam videtur haec quaestio mota fuisse, quia sine controversia et universaliter accepta erat consuetudo, veluti iure possessionis gaudens.

Ecclesiae ergo hac de re traditio per saecula tam firma fuit, ut magisterium numquam necesse habuerit edisserere principium, cui nulla labes inferebatur, seu legem defendere, quae nullo infitiante vigebat. At quotiescumque traditio illa, occasione data, manifestabatur, ea testimonio erat Ecclesiam in id intentam esse, ut ad exemplar sibi a Domino traditum se conformaret.

Eandem traditionem religiose custodierunt Orientales Ecclesiae, quarum unanimis hac de re consensus eo magis conspicuus est, quod de multis aliis rebus varium esse suum cuiusque ius libenter accipiant; atque etiam hodie quidquam commune habere recusant cum iis postulationibus, quibus mulierum sacerdotalis ordinatio intenditur.

II. QUOMODO CHRISTUS SE GESSERIT

Christus Iesus nullam mulierem inter Duodecim adscivit. Si ita se gessit, id non propterea evenit, quod sui temporis moribus cede-

---

[8] *Didascalia Apostolorum,* c. 15, ed. R. H. Connolly, pp. 133 et 142; *Constitutiones Apostolicae,* lib. 3, c. 6, nn. 1-2; C. 9, nn. 3-4: ed. F. X. Funk, pp. 191, 201; S. Ioannes Chrysostomus, *De sacerdotio,* 2, 2: PG 48, 633.

[9] S. Bonaventura, *In IV Sent.,* Dist. 25, art. 2, q. 1: ed. Quaracchi, t. 4, p. 649; Richardus de Mediavilla (Middletown), *In IV Sent.,* Dist. 25, art. 4, n. 1, ed. Venetiis 1499, f° 177ʳ; Ioannes Duns Scotus, *In IV Sent.,* Dist 25: *Opus Oxoniense,* ed. Vivès, t. 19, p. 140; *Reportata Parisiensia,* t. 24, pp. 369-371; Durandus a Sancto Porciano, *In IV Sent.,* Dist. 25, q. 2, ed. Venetiis 1571, f° 364ᵛ.

the Church intends to remain faithful to the type of ordained ministry willed by the Lord Jesus Christ and carefully maintained by the apostles.[8]

The same conviction animates medieval theology,[9] even if the scholastic doctors, in their desire to clarify by reason the data of faith, often present arguments on this point that modern thought would have difficulty in admitting or would even rightly reject. Since that period and up to our own time, it can be said that the question has not been raised again, for the practice has enjoyed peaceful and universal acceptance.

The Church's tradition in the matter has thus been so firm in the course of the centuries that the magisterium has not felt the need to intervene in order to formulate a principle which was not attacked, or to defend a law which was not challenged. But each time that this tradition had the occasion to manifest itself, it witnessed to the Church's desire to conform to the model left to her by the Lord.

The same tradition has been faithfully safeguarded by the Churches of the East. Their unanimity on this point is all the more remarkable since in many other questions their discipline admits of a great diversity. At the present time these same Churches refuse to associate themselves with requests directed towards securing the accession of women to priestly ordination.

II. THE ATTITUDE OF JESUS

Jesus Christ did not call any woman to become part of the Twelve. If he acted in this way, it was not in order to conform to the customs of his time, for his attitude towards women was quite different from that of his milieu, and he deliberately and courageously broke with it.

---

[8] *Didascalia Apostolorum*, ch. 15, ed. R. H. Connolly, pp. 133 and 142; *Constitutiones Apostolicae*, bk. 3, ch. 6, nos. 1-2; ch. 9, nos. 3-4: ed. F. H. Funk, pp. 191, 201; St. John Chrysostom, *De Sacerdotio* 2, 2: *PG* 48, 633.

[9] St. Bonaventure, *In IV Sent.*, Dist. 25, art. 2, q. 1, ed. Quaracchi, vol. 4, p. 649; Richard of Middleton, *In IV Sent.*, Dist. 25, art. 4, no. 1, ed. Venice, 1499, f 177; John Duns Scotus, *In IV Sent.*, Dist. 25: *Opus Oxoniense*, ed. Vives, vol. 19, p. 140; *Reportata Parisiensia*, vol. 24, pp. 369-371; Durandus of Saint-Pourcain, *In IV Sent.*, Dist. 25, q. 2, ed. Venice, 1571, f 364.

bat, nam ipsius cum mulieribus agendi ratio modo civium suorum prorsus dissimilis erat, et ab eorum observantia ille voluntarie audacterque se removebat. Sic nempe palam cum Samaritana muliere colloquitur, ideoque mirationem ipsis discipulis movet (cf *Io* 4,27); legalis immunditiae mulieris, quae sanguinis fluxum patiebatur, nullam rationem habet (cf *Mt* 9,20-22); a peccatrice muliere in domo Simonis pharisaei se tangi patitur (cf *Lc* 7,37 et ss.); mulierem in adulterio deprehensam absolvens, docere intendit haud severius agendum esse in mulierum quam in virorum culpas (cf *Io* 8,11); a lege Moysis se distineri non dubitans, aequalia asseverat viri ac mulieris quoad vinculum matrimonii iura et officia (cf *Mc* 10,2-11; *Mt* 19,3-9).

Cum vero iter faciens Iesus evangelizaret regnum Dei, sibi comites adiunxit non tantum Duodecim, sed etiam mulieres, inter quas erat *Maria, quae vocatur Magdalene, de qua daemonia septem exierant, et Ioanna uxor Chusa procuratoris Herodis, et Susanna, et aliae multae, quae ministrabant eis de facultatibus suis* (*Lc* 8,2-3).

Quamvis secundum mentis habitum Hebraeum haud magni valoris esset, teste iure Iudaico, mulieris testimonium, tamen primae Dominum a mortuis suscitatum viderunt mulieres, et ille iis officium commisit primum paschale nuntium Apostolis ipsis afferendi (cf *Mt* 28,7-10; *Lc* 24,9-10; *Io* 20,11-18), qui praepararentur, ut publici Resurrectionis testes postea fierent.

Haec vero omnia — id fatendum est — non quidem talem evidentiam afferunt, ut cuique proxime perspicua sint, quod quidem mirandum non est, siquidem quaestiones, quas movet Verbum Dei, altiores sunt quam ut responsa pateant; nam ad intellegendum tam Iesu missionis, quam Scripturae ipsius ultimum sensum, non satis est mere historicam textuum enarrationem instruere. Hac tamen in re agnoscendus est velut fascis colligatus factorum, quae in idem indicandum vergunt, magisque admirationem movent quod Iesus munus apostolicum [10] mulieribus non concredidit. Ipsa Mater eius, Filii

---

[10] Obiciunt quidam Iesum ideo duodecim viros elegisse, ut signum allegoricum compleret, quippe qui in figura significaret, hos duodecim eorum personam acturos qui duodecim tribus Israel genuerant (cf *Mt* 19,28; *Lc* 22,30). At in textibus ad id allatis nil asseritur nisi duodecim in iudicio eschatologico partem habituros. Genuina ratio,

For example, to the great astonishment of his own disciples Jesus converses publicly with the Samaritan woman (cf. Jn 4:27); he takes no notice of the state of legal impurity of the woman who had suffered from hemorrhages (cf. Mt 9:20-22); he allows a sinful woman to approach him in the house of Simon the Pharisee (cf. Lk 7:37ff); and by pardoning the woman taken in adultery, he means to show that one must not be more severe towards the fault of a woman than towards that of a man (cf. Jn 8:11). He does not hesitate to depart from the Mosaic law in order to affirm the equality of the rights and duties of men and women with regard to the marriage bond (cf. Mk 10:2-11; Mt 19:3-9).

In his itinerant ministry Jesus was accompanied not only by the Twelve but also by a group of women: "Mary, surnamed the Magdalene, from whom seven demons had gone out, Joanna the wife of Herod's steward Chuza, Susanna, and several others who provided for them out of their own resources" (Lk 8:2-3). Contrary to the Jewish mentality, which did not accord great value to the testimony of women, as Jewish law attests, it was nevertheless women who were the first to have the privilege of seeing the risen Lord, and it was they who were charged by Jesus to take the first paschal message to the apostles themselves (cf. Mt 28:7-10; Lk 24:9-10; Jn 20:11-18), in order to prepare the latter to become the official witnesses to the resurrection.

It is true that these facts do not make the matter immediately obvious. This is no surprise, for the questions that the word of God brings before us go beyond the obvious. In order to reach the ultimate meaning of the mission of Jesus and the ultimate meaning of scripture, a purely historical exegesis of the texts cannot suffice.

But it must be recognized that we have here a number of convergent indications that make all the more remarkable the fact that Jesus did not entrust the apostolic charge[10] to women. Even his mother, who was so closely associated with the mystery of her Son, and whose incomparable role is emphasized by the Gospels of Luke and John, was not invested with the apostolic ministry.

---

[10] Some have also wished to explain this fact by a symbolic intention of Jesus: the Twelve were to represent the ancestors of the twelve tribes of Israel (cf. Mt 19:28; Lk 22:30). But in these texts it is only a question of their participation in the eschatological

mysterio tam arcte sociata, cuius partes eximiae in Lucae et Ioannis Evangeliis extolluntur, apostolico non est affecta ministerio. Quod Patres induxit, ut Mariam in exemplum proponerent Christi hac in re voluntatis: eandemque doctrinam, saeculo ineunte XIII, adhuc confirmavit Innocentius Pp. III, scribens: *Licet beatissima Virgo Maria dignior et excellentior fuerit Apostolis universis, non tamen illi, sed istis Dominus claves regni coelorum commisit.*[11]

III. APOSTOLI QUOMODO SE GESSERINT

Hunc Christi modum cum mulieribus agendi Apostolica communitas fideliter observavit. Etsi B. Maria insignem locum obtinebat inter illos paucos, qui in Cenaculum post Domini ascensionem congregabantur (cf *Act* 1,14), non tamen ipsa in Collegium duodecim Apostolorum est cooptata, cum de electione ageretur, cuius exitus fuit designatio Matthiae; duo enim discipuli propositi erant, de quorum nominibus Evangelia ne mentionem quidem faciunt.

Die autem Pentecostes, Spiritu Sancto repleti sunt omnes, viri ac mulieres (cf *Act* 2,1; 1,14), attamen nonnisi *Petrus cum undecim levavit vocem suam,* ut nuntiaret in Iesu adimpletas esse prophetias (*Act* 2,14).

Illis vero atque Paulo, quando terminos orbis Iudaeorum transierunt, necesse fuit, ut Evangelium et vitam christianam hominibus Graeco et Romano cultu atque humanitate imbutis praedicarent, Mosaicae Legis observantias solvere, et quidem interdum cum dolore. Potuissent ergo, nisi iis persuasum esset in hoc fidem Christo servandam esse, libenter sibi proponere, ut mulieribus ordinem conferrent. Apud illius aetatis Graecos plura quorundam deorum sacri-

---

cur Duodecim electi sint, intellegitur potius ex toto illorum munere, ad quod vocati sunt (cf *Mc* 3,14), ut scilicet Christum in populo repraesentarent eiusque opus continuarent.

[11] INNOCENTIUS PP. III, *Epist.* 11 decembris 1210 ad episcopos Palentin. et Burgen., in *Corpore Iuris, Decretal.* lib. 5, tit. 38, *De paenit.* c. 10 *Nova:* ed. A. Friedberg, t. 2, col. 886-887; cf *Glossa in Decretal.* lib. 1, tit. 33, c. 12 *Dilecta, v° Iurisdictioni.* Cf S. THOMAS, *Summ. theol.,* III^a pars, quaest. 27, art. 5, ad 3um; PSEUDO-ALBERTUS MAGNUS *Mariale,* quaest. 42: ed. Borgnet 37, 81.

This fact was to lead the fathers to present her as the example of Christ's will in this domain; as Pope Innocent III repeated later, at the beginning of the thirteenth century, "Although the Blessed Virgin Mary surpassed in dignity and in excellence all the apostles, nevertheless it was not to her but to them that the Lord entrusted the keys of the kingdom of heaven."[11]

III. THE PRACTICE OF THE APOSTLES

The apostolic community remained faithful to the attitude of Jesus towards women. Although Mary occupied a privileged place in the little circle of those gathered in the upper room after the Lord's ascension (cf. Acts 1:14), it was not she who was called to enter the college of the Twelve at the time of the election that resulted in the choice of Matthias: those who were put forward were two disciples whom the Gospels do not even mention.

On the day of Pentecost, the Holy Spirit filled them all, men and women (cf. Acts 2:1; 1:14), yet the proclamation of the fulfillment of the prophecies in Jesus was made only by "Peter and the eleven" (Acts 2:14).

When they and Paul went beyond the confines of the Jewish world, the preaching of the Gospel and the Christian life in the Greco-Roman civilization impelled them to break with Mosaic practices, sometimes regretfully. They could therefore have envisaged conferring ordination on women, if they had not been convinced of their duty of fidelity to the Lord on this point.

In the Hellenistic world, the cult of a number of pagan divinities was entrusted to priestesses. In fact the Greeks did not share the ideas of the Jews: although their philosophers taught the inferiority of women,

---

judgment. The essential meaning of the choice of the Twelve should rather be sought in the totality of their mission (cf. Mk 3:14): they are to represent Jesus to the people and carry on his work.

[11] Pope Innocent III, *Epist.* (December 11, 1210) to the bishops of Palencia and Burgos, included in *Corpus Iuris, Decret. Lib.* 5, tit. 38, *De Paenit.*, ch. 10 *Nova:* ed A. Friedberg, vol. 2, col. 886-887; cf. *Glossa in Decretal. Lib.* 1, tit. 33, ch. 12 *Dilecta, v Iurisdictioni.* Cf. St. Thomas, *Summa Theologiae*, III, q. 27, a. 5 ad 3; Pseudo-Albert the Great, *Mariale*, quaest. 42, ed. Borgnet 37, 81.

ficia exstabant, quae per mulieres confici solerent. Graeci enim a Iudaeorum opinionibus aberant: etsi eorum philosophi mulierem viro inferiorem esse profitebantur, fiebant inter eos ad promovendam aliquo modo mulierum dignitatem concitationes, quas historiarum scriptores notatu dignas aestimant, quaeque imperatorum temporibus creverunt. Revera ex libro Actuum Apostolorum atque Epistulis beati Pauli constat mulieres quasdam cum Apostolo in Evangelio laborasse (cf *Rom* 16,3-12; *Phil* 4,3); et ille gratus singularum nomina enumerat inter salutationes, quibus Epistulas suas concludit; ad conversiones promovendas partes haud parvas habuerunt quaedam ex illis mulieribus, ut Priscilla, Lydia, aliaeque; prae ceteris vero Priscilla, nam *Priscilla et Aquila assumpserunt Apollo et diligentius exposuerunt ei viam Dei* (cf *Act* 18,26); Phoebe etiam, quae erat *ministra Ecclesiae quae est Cenchris* (*Rom* 16,1). Ex his omnibus manifeste constat mores Ecclesiae Apostolorum longe a Iudaeorum moribus recessisse; attamen numquam mulieribus illis ordinationem conferre cogitaverunt.

In Pauli Epistulis, probati exegetae animadverterunt varios esse dicendi modos ab Apostolo usurpatos; scribens enim *adiutores meos* (*Rom* 16,3; *Phil* 4,2-3), nominat indistincte viros et mulieres, qui quocumque titulo eum in Evangelio adiuvant; nomen vero Dei adiutores (*1 Cor* 3,9; cf *1 Thess* 3,2) reservat Apollo, Timotheo sibique Paulo, utpote qui directe ad apostolicum ministerium et verbi Dei praedicationem segregati sint. Mulierum tamen quamvis insigne fuisset die Resurrectionis munus, cooperatio ad id a Paulo non extensa est, ut illo publico munere sollemniter praeconium nuntiandi fungerentur, quod unius missionis apostolicae proprium est.

IV. QUAE CHRISTUS ET APOSTOLI FECERUNT, NORMA SUNT PERPETUA

Etsi hic Christi et Apostolorum modus se gerendi a tota persaecula usque ad nos firma traditione ut norma habitus est, quaestio tamen oritur, num hodie aliter se gerere Ecclesiae liceat. Sunt qui affirmative respondeant, pluribus rationibus fulti, quas pervestigare oportet.

historians nevertheless emphasize the existence of a certain movement for the advancement of women during the imperial period.

In fact we know from the book of the Acts and from the Letters of St. Paul that certain women worked with the apostle for the Gospel (cf. Rom 16:3-12; Phil 4:3). St. Paul lists their names with gratitude in the final salutations of the letters. Some of them often exercised an important influence on conversions: Priscilla, Lydia, and others; especially Priscilla, who took it on herself to complete the instruction of Apollos (cf. Acts 18:26); Phoebe, in the service of the Church of Cenchreae (cf. Rom 16:1). All these facts manifest within the apostolic Church a considerable evolution vis-a-vis the customs of Judaism. Nevertheless at no time was there a question of conferring ordination on these women.

In the Pauline letters, exegetes of authority have noted a difference between two formulas used by the apostle: he writes indiscriminately "my fellow workers" (Rom 16:3; Phil 4:2-3) when referring to men and women helping him in his apostolate in one way or another; but he reserves the title "God's fellow workers" (1 Cor 3:9; cf. 1 Thess 3:2) to Apollos, Timothy, and himself, thus designated because they are directly set apart for the apostolic ministry and the preaching of the word of God. In spite of the so important role played by women on the day of the resurrection, their collaboration was not extended by St. Paul to the official and public proclamation of the message, since this proclamation belongs exclusively to the apostolic mission.

IV. PERMANENT VALUE OF THE ATTITUDE OF JESUS AND THE APOSTLES

Could the Church today depart from this attitude of Jesus and the apostles, which has been considered as normative by the whole of tradition up to our own day? Various arguments have been put forward in favor of a positive reply to this question, and these must now be examined.

It has been claimed in particular that the attitude of Jesus and the apostles is explained by the influence of their milieu and their times. It is said that, if Jesus did not entrust to women and not even to his mother

Asseverant praesertim Iesum et Apostolos sic egisse, quia mores illius temporis regionisque necessario observabant, nec aliam causam fuisse, cur Christus ministerium neque mulieribus neque ipsi Matri suae committeret, nisi quod aliter agere prohiberent eiusdem temporis adiuncta. Nemo tamen probavit, ac reapse probari non potest, eiusmodi agendi modum solum a rationibus socialibus et cultus humani propriis esse profectum. Revera, cum Evangelia supra examinaremus, Iesum contra conspeximus ab opinionibus suorum coaetaneorum se longe distraxisse, ea auferendo discrimina, quibus mulieres a viris separabantur. Asseverari ergo non potest Iesum opportunitatis tantum rationem habuisse, cum mulieres in apostolicum coetum non adnumeraret. Eo minus Apostoli ad hunc morem observandum societatis cultusque adiunctis coacti sunt apud Graecos, quod illi haec discrimina ignorabant.

Praeterea obiciunt, inter ea, quae Paulus de mulieribus praescripsit, nonnulla esse, quae nostris temporibus caduca censeantur, atque partes aliquas eius doctrinae difficultates movere. At contra animadvertendum est fere omnia praecepta illa, ut veri simile esse videtur, ab aetatis moribus petita, ad disciplinae nonnisi minoris momenti usus spectare, cuiusmodi est obligatio facta mulieribus caput velandi (cf *1 Cor* 11,2-16); quae praescripta iam non urgent. Cum vero Paulus, ut mulieres in ecclesia taceant statuit, non permittens eas loqui (*1 Cor* 14,34-35; cf *1 Tim* 2,12), haec interdictio diversae est indolis eiusque significationem exegetae illustrant, nempe apostolum mulieribus non adimere ius, quod aliunde agnoscit, in ecclesia prophetandi (cf *1 Cor* 11,5), sed solum prohibere, ne publicum docendi munus gerant in coetu christiano. Haec interdictio secundum Paulum cum consilio divino de creatione conectitur (cf *1 Cor* 11,7; *Gen* 2,18-24), nec facile cultui moribusque adscribenda est. Praeterea in mentem revocare iuvat Paulum eum fuisse, qui in Novi Testamenti scriptis, de primi iuris virorum et mulierum aequalitate, utpote Dei filiorum in Christo (cf *Gal* 3,28), maxima cum firmitate diceret. Nihil denique est, cur Paulus accusetur infensorum praeiudiciorum in mulieres, quibus ex contrario eum fiduciam significasse quasque ad laborandum secum vocasse constet.

a ministry assimilating them to the Twelve, this was because historical circumstances did not permit him to do so.

No one however has ever proved—and it is clearly impossible to prove—that this attitude is inspired only by social and cultural reasons. As we have seen, an examination of the Gospels shows on the contrary that Jesus broke with the prejudices of his time, by widely contravening the discriminations practiced with regard to women. One therefore cannot maintain that, by not calling women to enter the group of the apostles, Jesus was simply letting himself be guided by reasons of expediency.

For all the more reason, social and cultural conditioning did not hold back the apostles working in the Greek milieu, where the same forms of discrimination did not exist.

Another objection is based upon the transitory character that one claims to see today in some of the prescriptions of St. Paul concerning women, and upon the difficulties that some aspects of his teaching raise in this regard. But it must be noted that these ordinances, probably inspired by the customs of the period, concern scarcely more than disciplinary practices of minor importance, such as the obligation imposed upon women to wear a veil on the head (1 Cor 11:2-16); such requirements no longer have a normative value.

However, the apostle's forbidding of women "to speak" in the assemblies (cf. 1 Cor 14:34-35; 1 Tim 2:12) is of a different nature, and exegetes define its meaning in this way: Paul in no way opposes the right, which he elsewhere recognizes as possessed by women, to prophesy in the assembly (cf. 1 Cor 11:5); the prohibition solely concerns the official function of teaching in the Christian assembly. For St. Paul this prescription is bound up with the divine plan of creation (cf. 1 Cor 11:7; Gen 2:18-24): it would be difficult to see in it the expression of a cultural fact.

Nor should it be forgotten that we owe to St. Paul one of the most vigorous texts in the New Testament on the fundamental equality of men and women, as children of God in Christ (cf. Gal 3:28). Therefore there is no reason for accusing him of prejudices against women, when we note the trust that he shows towards them and the collaboration that he asks of them in his apostolate.

Ad haec vero de apostolicae aetatis adiunctis obiecta addunt, qui legitimam futuram esse huiusmodi disciplinae mutationem contendunt, considerandum esse, quomodo Ecclesia sacramentorum disciplinam moderetur. Equidem animadvertitur, nostris praecipue temporibus, quam conscia sit Ecclesia se in sacramenta, quamvis a Christo instituta, potestate quadam pollere, cuius decursu temporum usa est, ut eorum signum distinctius designaret, atque ea ministrandi condiciones determinaret; quod patet ex recentibus Summorum Pontificum Pii XII Paulique VI decretis.[12] Attamen sedulo advertendum est hanc potestatem, quamvis veram, certis finibus circumscriptam esse. De hoc monuit Pius Papa XII scribens: *Ecclesiae nulla competit potestas in substantiam Sacramentorum, id est in ea quae, testibus divinae revelationis fontibus, ipse Christus Dominus in signo Sacramenti servanda statuit.*[13] Quae iam docuit Tridentina Synodus declarans: *Hanc potestatem perpetuo in Ecclesia fuisse, ut in Sacramentorum dispensatione, salva illorum substantia, ea statueret vel mutaret, quae suscipientium utilitati seu ipsorum Sacramentorum venerationi, pro rerum, temporum et locorum varietate, magis expedire iudicaret.*[14]

Praeterea haud praetermittendum est sacramentalia signa non, quasi ex pacto convenerit, selecta esse: non solum sub multiplici respectu, signa sunt reapse naturalia, utpote quae gestuum, rerumque vim significandi naturaliter inditam assumant, sed praecipue ordinantur ad annectendos illi summo, qui praecesserit, salutis eventui posterioris aetatis homines, eosque uberi sacrorum Bibliorum vi educandos et arte symbolica docendos, qualem gratiam significent atque efficiant. Sic Sacramentum Eucharistiae non est mere fraternum convivium, sed simul memoriale praesens et *actuale* denuo faciens Christi sacrificium, nec non eius ab Ecclesia facta oblatio; sic ministeriale sacerdotium non est tantum pastorale munus, sed continuationem infert eorum munerum, quae Apostolis Christus concredidit, potestatumque, quae ad ea munera pertinent. Aptatio ergo ad

---

[12] Pius PP XII, Constit. Apost. *Sacramentum Ordinis,* 30 novembris 1917: AAS 40 (1948), pp. 5-7; Paulus PP. VI, Const. Apost. *Divinae Consortium Naturae,* 15 augusti 1971: AAS 63 (1971), pp. 657-664; Const. Apost. *Sacram Unctionem,* 30 novembris 1972: AAS 65 (1973), pp. 5-9.

[13] Pius PP. XII, Const. Apost. *Sacramentum Ordinis: loc. cit.,* p. 5.

[14] Sessio 21, cap. 2: Denzinger-Schönmetzer, *Enchiridion symbolorum...,* n. 1728.

But over and above these objections taken from the history of apostolic times, those who support the legitimacy of change in the matter turn to the Church's practice in her sacramental discipline. It has been noted, in our day especially, to what extent the Church is conscious of possessing a certain power over the sacraments, even though they were instituted by Christ. She has used this power down the centuries in order to determine their signs and the conditions of their administration: recent decisions of Popes Pius XII and Paul VI are proof of this.[12]

However, it must be emphasized that this power, which is a real one, has definite limits. As Pope Pius XII recalled: "The Church has no power over the substance of the sacraments, that is to say, over what Christ the Lord, as the sources of revelation bear witness, determined should be maintained in the sacramental sign."[13] This was already the teaching of the Council of Trent, which declared: "In the Church there has always existed this power, that in the administration of the sacraments, provided that their substance remains unaltered, she can lay down or modify what she considers more fitting either for the benefit of those who receive them or for respect towards those same sacraments, according to varying circumstances, times or places."[14]

Moreover, it must not be forgotten that the sacramental signs are not conventional ones. Not only is it true that, in many respects, they are natural signs because they respond to the deep symbolism of actions and things, but they are more than this: they are principally meant to link the person of every period to the supreme event of the history of salvation, in order to enable that person to understand, through all the Bible's wealth of pedagogy and symbolism, what grace they signify and produce.

For example, the sacrament of the eucharist is not only a fraternal meal, but at the same time the memorial that makes present and

---

[12] Pope Pius XII, apostolic constitution *Sacramentum Ordinis*, November 30, 1947: *AAS* 40 (1948), pp. 5-7; Pope Paul VI, apostolic constitution *Divinae Consortium Naturae*, August 15, 1971: *AAS* 63 (1971), pp. 657-664; apostolic constitution *Sacram Unctionem*, November 30, 1972: *AAS* 65 (1973), pp. 5- 9.

[13] Pope Pius XII, apostolic constitution *Sacramentum Ordinis: loc. cit.,* p. 5.

[14] Session 21, chap. 2: Denzinger-Schonmetzer, *Enchiridion Symbolorum* 1728.

tempora civilisque cultus formas ad id extendi nequit, ut solvatur quoad substantiam hoc sacramentale vinculum cum iis eventibus, qui christianam religionem fundaverunt, et cum Christo ipso.

His in rebus, ad extremum est Ecclesiae, per suum Magisterium pronuntiantis, decernere quaenam partes sint immutabiles, quae vero ·partes mutationi sint obnoxiae. Ideo Ecclesia certas mutationes haud sibi admittendas esse censet, quia conscia est se Christi modo agendi obstrictam esse: tunc multum abest, ut moveatur antiquitatis fallaci studio, sed revera Domino suo servat fidem, cuius sola luce vera ratio eius iudicii intellegi potest. Ecclesia autem sententiam suam dicit, innixa in Domini promisso nec non in Spiritus Sancti praesentia, atque eo consilio, quo luculentius annuntietur Christi mysterium maioreque sedulitate custodiantur et ostendantur integrae eius divitiae.

Ecclesiae ergo praxis vim normae habet. In eo autem quod solum viris ordinatio sacerdotalis confertur, subest traditio continua per totam Ecclesiae historiam, universalis tam in Oriente quam in Occidente, intenta ad pravos usus statim coercendos; quae norma, exemplo Christi innixa, ideo observata est, et observatur, quia putatur conformis esse proposito Dei circa Ecclesiam suam.

V. MINISTERIALE SACERDOTIUM MYSTERII CHRISTI LUCE CONTEMPLANDUM EST

Postquam haec Ecclesiae norma huiusque fundamentum in mentem revocata sunt, utile et opportunum videtur eandem normam illustrare ostendendo eius, quam theologica cogitatio dignoscit, convenientiam: quod enim nonnisi viri ad ordinationem sacerdotalem accipiendam vocati sunt, hoc arcte convenit cum Sacramenti genuina indole eiusque specifica ad Christi mysterium relatione. Tunc vero non intenditur, ut argumentum demonstrativum afferatur, sed ut doctrina per analogiam fidei illustretur.

Constans Ecclesiae doctrina est, quam denuo fusiusque declaravit Concilium Vaticanum II, revocavit etiam Synodus Episcoporum anno 1971 habita, iteravit denique Sacra haec Congregatio pro Doctrina Fidei in sua die 24 Iunii anno 1973 data Declaratione, Episcopum vel Presbyterum, suo quemque munere fungentem, in persona

actual Christ's sacrifice and his offering by the Church. Again, the priestly ministry is not just a pastoral service; it ensures the continuity of the functions entrusted by Christ to the apostles and the continuity of the powers related to those functions. Adaptation to civilizations and times therefore cannot abolish, on essential points, the sacramental reference to constitutive events of Christianity and to Christ himself.

In the final analysis it is the Church, through the voice of her magisterium, that, in these various domains, decides what can change and what must remain immutable. When she judges that she cannot accept certain changes, it is because she knows that she is bound by Christ's manner of acting. Her attitude, despite appearances, is therefore not one of archaism but of fidelity: it can be truly understood only in this light. The Church makes pronouncements in virtue of the Lord's promise and the presence of the Holy Spirit, in order to proclaim better the mystery of Christ and to safeguard and manifest the whole of its rich content.

This practice of the Church therefore has a normative character: in the fact of conferring priestly ordination only on men, it is a question of an unbroken tradition throughout the history of the Church, universal in the East and in the West, and alert to repress abuses immediately. This norm, based on Christ's example, has been and is still observed because it is considered to conform to God's plan for his Church.

V. THE MINISTERIAL PRIESTHOOD IN THE LIGHT OF THE MYSTERY OF CHRIST

Having recalled the Church's norm and the basis thereof, it seems useful and opportune to illustrate this norm by showing the profound fittingness that theological reflection discovers between the proper nature of the sacrament of order, with its specific reference to the mystery of Christ, and the fact that only men have been called to receive priestly ordination. It is not a question here of bringing forward a demonstrative argument, but of clarifying this teaching by the analogy of faith.

The Church's constant teaching, repeated and clarified by the Second Vatican Council and again recalled by the 1971 Synod of Bishops

propria non agere, sed Christum repraesentare, qui per eum agit: *sacerdos vice Christi vere fungitur,* ut scripsit iam saeculo III S. Cyprianus.[15] Christum ipsum repraesentare posse, hoc Paulus proprium esse affirmavit apostolici sui muneris (cf *2 Cor* 5,20; *Gal* 4, 14). Quae Christi repraesentatio tunc altissimam sui significationem ac peculiarem prorsus modum assequitur, cum eucharistica celebratur synaxis, fons et centrum Ecclesiae unitatis, convivium sacrificale, quo populus Dei sacrificio Christi coniungitur: sacerdos, qui solus potestatem habet id perficiendi, agit non tantum virtute, quae ei a Christo confertur, sed in persona Christi,[16] huius partes sustinens, ita ut ipsam eius imaginem gerat, cum verba consecrationis enuntiat.[17]

Christianum ergo sacerdotium est sacramentalis indolis, sacerdos est signum, cuius quidem supernaturalis efficacitas ordinatione accepta obtinetur, at signum, quod percipi oportet,[18] cuiusque significationem fideles facile dignoscant. Tota enim sacramentorum oeconomia in signis naturalibus fundatur, quae vim significandi habent cum hominum animo concinentem: *signa sacramentalia,* ut ait S. Thomas, *ex naturali similitudine repraesentant.*[19] Eadem autem naturalis similitudo exigitur circa personas, quae circa res: cum enim re-

---

[15] S. Cyprianus, *Epist.* 63, 14: *PL* 4, 397 B; ed. Hartel, t. 3, p. 713.

[16] Conc. Oec. Vat. II, Constit. *Sacrosanctum Concilium,* 4 decembris 1963, n. 33 *...a sacerdote, qui coetui in persona Christi praeest...;* Constit, dogmat. *Lumen Gentium,* 21 novembris 1964, n. 10: *sacerdos quidem ministerialis, potestate sacra qua gaudet, populum sacerdotalem efformat ac regit, sacrificium eucharisticum in persona Christi conficit illudque nomine totius populi Deo offert...;* n. 28: *vi sacramenti Ordinis, ad imaginem Christi, summi atque aeterni Sacerdotis... suum munus sacrum maxime exercent in eucharistico cultu vel synaxi, qua in persona Christi agentes...;* Decret. *Presbyterorum Ordinis,* 7 decembris 1965, n. 2: *... Presbyteri, unctione Spiritus Sancti, speciali charactere signantur et sic Christo Sacerdoti configurantur, ita ut in persona Christi Capitis agere valeant;* n. 13: *ut sacrorum ministri, praesertim in sacrificio missae, presbyteri personam specialiter gerunt Christi...;* cf Synodus Episcoporum a. 1971, *De sacerdotio ministeriali,* I, 4; S. Congr. pro Doctrina Fidei, *Declaratio circa catholicam doctrinam de Ecclesia,* 24 iunii 1973, n. 6.

[17] S. Thomas, *Summ. theol.,* III[a] pars, quaest. 83, art. 1, ad 3[um]; *Dicendum est quod* [sicut celebratio huius sacramenti est imago repraesentativa crucis ipsius: *ibid.* ad 2[um]], *per eandem rationem etiam sacerdos gerit imaginem Christi, in cuius persona et virtute verba pronunciat ad consecrandum.*

[18] *Quia cum sacramentum sit signum in eis quae in sacramento aguntur, requiritur non solum res, sed significatio rei,* ait S. Thomas plane ad ordinationem mulierum removendam: *In IV Sent.,* dist. 25, q. 2, art. 1, quaestiuncula 1[a] corp.

[19] S. Thomas, *In IV Sent.,* dist. 25, q. 2, art. 2, quaestiuncula 1[a], ad 4[um].

and by the Sacred Congregation for the Doctrine of the Faith in its declaration of June 24, 1973, declares that the bishop or the priest, in the exercise of his ministry, does not act in his own name, *in persona propria:* he represents Christ, who acts through him: "the priest truly acts in the place of Christ," as St. Cyprian already wrote in the third century.[15]

It is this ability to represent Christ that St. Paul considered as characteristic of his apostolic function (cf. 2 Cor 5:20; Gal 4:14). The supreme expression of this representation is found in the altogether special form it assumes in the celebration of the eucharist, which is the source and center of the Church's unity, the sacrificial meal in which the people of God are associated in the sacrifice of Christ: the priest, who alone has the power to perform it, then acts not only through the effective power conferred on him by Christ, but in *persona Christi*,[16] taking the role of Christ, to the point of being his very image, when he pronounces the words of consecration.[17]

The Christian priesthood is therefore of a sacramental nature: the priest is a sign, the supernatural effectiveness of which comes from the

---

[15] St. Cyprian, *Epist.* 63, 14: *PL* 4, 397 B; ed. Hartel, vol. 3, p. 713.

[16] Second Vatican Council, constitution *Sacrosanctum Concilium*, 33 (December 4, 1963): ". . . by the priest who presides over the assembly in the person of Christ. . ."; dogmatic constitution *Lumen Gentium*, 10 (November 21, 1964): "The ministerial priest, by the sacred power he enjoys, molds and rules the priestly people. Acting in the person of Christ, he brings about the eucharistic sacrifice, and offers it to God in the name of all the people. . ."; 28: "By the powers of the sacrament of order, and in the image of Christ the eternal high priest . . . they exercise this sacred function of Christ above all in the eucharistic liturgy or synaxis. There, acting in the person of Christ. . ."; decree *Presbyterorum Ordinis,* 2 (December 7, 1965): ". . . priests, by the anointing of the Holy Spirit, are marked with a special character and are so configured to Christ the priest that they can act in the person of Christ the head"; 13: "As ministers of sacred realities, especially in the sacrifice of the Mass, priests represent the person of Christ in a special way"; cf. 1971 Synod of Bishops, *De Sacerdotio Ministeriali* I, 4; Sacred Congregation for the Doctrine of the Faith, *Declaratio circa catholicam doctrinam de Ecclesia*, 6 (June 24, 1973).

[17] St. Thomas, *Summa Theologiae*, III q. 83, art. 1, ad 3: "It is to be said that just as the celebration of this sacrament is the representative image of Christ's cross (ibid, ad 2), for the same reason the priest also enacts the image of Christ, in whose person and by whose power he pronounces the words of consecration."

praesentare oportet sacramentaliter Christi agendi modum in Eucharistia, non haberetur haec naturalis similitudo, quae inter Christum eiusque ministrum postulatur, nisi partes a viro agerentur: secus difficile in eodem ministro imago Christi perspiceretur; siquidem Christus ipse fuit et permanet vir.

Sine dubio totius generis humani mulierum aeque ac virorum primogenitus est Christus: unitatem peccato fractam ita reparavit, ut iam non sit Iudaeus neque Graecus, non sit servus neque liber, non masculus et femina: omnes enim unus sunt in Christo Iesu (cf *Gal* 3,28). Attamen Verbum incarnatum est secundum sexum virilem; quae quidem res in facto innititur, quod, nedum excellentiam quandam viri super mulierem importet, ab oeconomia salutis seiungi non potest: etenim id cum universo consilio Dei consonat — sicut a Deo est revelatum — cuius nucleus est Foederis mysterium.

Salus enim, quae hominibus a Deo offertur, seu unio cum eo, ad quam vocantur, Foedus nempe, describebatur iam in Vetere Testamento, apud Prophetas, praecipue sub figura nuptialis mysterii: populum electum fieri Dei sponsam ardenter dilectam; cuius dilectionis familiaritatem intimam traditio cum Iudaea tum christiana pervidit, quae iterum iterumque Cantica Canticorum perlegebat; sponsum vero fidelem mansurum esse, etiam quoties sponsa amorem eius deciperet, id est quoties Israel Deo infidelis esset (cf *Os* 1-3; *Ier* 2). At ubi venit plenitudo temporis (*Gal* 4,4), Verbum, Dei Filius, ideo caro factum est, ut iniret et sanciret novum et aeternum Testamentum in sanguine suo, qui pro multis effunderetur in remissionem peccatorum: cuius mors filios Dei, qui erant dispersi, congregaret in unum; cuius e latere transfixo Ecclesia nascitur, sicut Eva e latere Adam est nata. Tunc plenum et sempiternum efficitur hoc nuptiarum mysterium, quod nuntiaverunt atque cecinerunt scripta Veteris Testamenti: Christus est sponsus; Ecclesia est eius sponsa, quam ideo diligit, quod eam acquisivit sanguine suo, ut eam exhiberet sibi gloriosam, sanctam et immaculatam, neque ab ea iam separari potest. Argumentum nempe nuptiarum evolvitur inde ab Epistulis sancti Pauli (cf *2 Cor* 11,2; *Eph* 5,22-33) usque ad beati Ioannis scripta (praecipue *Io* 3,29; *Apoc* 19,7 et 9); innuitur vero etiam in synopticis Evangeliis, nam *quanto tempore habent secum sponsum, non possunt ieiunare amici eius* (cf *Mc* 2,19); simile factum

ordination received, but a sign that must be perceptible[18] and which the faithful must be able to recognize with ease.

The whole sacramental economy is in fact based upon natural signs, on symbols imprinted upon the human psychology: "Sacramental signs," says St. Thomas, "represent what they signify by natural resemblance."[19]

The same natural resemblance is required for persons as for things: when Christ's role in the eucharist is to be expressed sacramentally, there would not be this "natural resemblance" which must exist between Christ and his minister if the role of Christ were not taken by a man: in such a case it would be difficult to see in the minister the image of Christ. For Christ himself was and remains a man.

Christ is of course the firstborn of all humanity, of women as well as men: the unity which he re-established after sin is such that there are no more distinctions between Jew and Greek, slave and free, male and female, but all are one in Christ Jesus (cf. Gal 3:28). Nevertheless, the incarnation of the word took place according to the male sex: this is indeed a question of fact, and this fact, while not implying an alleged natural superiority of man over woman, cannot be disassociated from the economy of salvation: it is, indeed, in harmony with the entirety of God's plan as God himself has revealed it, and of which the mystery of the covenant is the nucleus.

For the salvation offered by God to men and women, the union with him to which they are called—in short, the covenant—took on, from the Old Testament prophets onwards, the privileged form of a nuptial mystery: for God the chosen people is seen as his ardently loved spouse.

Both Jewish and Christian tradition have discovered the depth of this intimacy of love by reading and rereading the Song of Songs; the divine bridegroom will remain faithful even when the bride betrays his love, when Israel is unfaithful to God (cf. Hos 1-3; Jer 2).

---

[18] "For since a sacrament is a sign, there is required in the things that are done in the sacraments not only the 'res' but the signification of the 'res,'" recalls St. Thomas, precisely in order to reject the ordination of women: *In IV Sent.*, dist. 25, q. 2, art. 1, quaestiuncula 1, corp.

[19] St. Thomas, *In IV Sent.*, dist. 25, q. 2, quaestiuncula 1 ad 4.

est Regnum caelorum homini regi qui fecit nuptias filio suo (*Mt* 22, 1-14). Sermone illo Sacrae Scripturae, symbolis intertexto, quo vir et mulier in intima sua identitate exprimuntur et attinguntur, revelatum est nobis mysterium Dei et Christi, quod ex se pervestigari non potest.

Numquam ergo praetermittendum est Christum virum esse. Ideo, ne momentum huiusmodi symbolismi neglegatur in oeconomia Revelationis, tenendum est in iis actionibus, quae ordinationis characterem postulant et in quibus repraesentatur Christus ipse, auctor Foederis, sponsus et caput Ecclesiae, suo salutis officio fungens, quod praeclarissimo modo in Eucharistia fieri contingit, partes eius — haec est enim primigenia significatio verbi « personae » — viro agendas esse. Hoc vero in viro nequaquam oritur ab aliqua excellentia, quatenus est persona, in ordine valorum, sed solum a diversitate, quae, in ordine munerum et servitii rationum, in factis innititur.

Num dici potest, cum Christus sit nunc in caelesti condicione, iam nihil interesse, utrum a viro an a muliere repraesentetur, quia *in resurrectione neque nubent neque nubentur* (*Mt* 22,30)? Haec tamen verba non significant viri ac mulieris distinctionem in aeterna gloria aboleri, cum identitatem personae propriam determinent. Quod de Christo dicendum est sicut de nobis. Plane enim compertum est sexus diversitatem in natura humana magnum influxum exercere, utique profundiorem quam exempli causa gentium diversitates; hae enim non tam intime humanam personam afficiunt quam sexus diversitas, quae directe ordinatur cum ad personarum communionem, tum ad humanam generationem, atque in revelatione biblica ascribitur primordiali Dei voluntati: *masculum et feminam creavit eos* (*Gen* 1,27).

Attamen, instabunt aliqui forsan dicentes sacerdotem, maxime cum liturgicis et sacramentalibus actionibus praesideat, pariter Ecclesiam repraesentare, utpote cuius nomine agat, intendens « facere id quod facit Ecclesia ». Eo nempe sensu aetatis mediae theologi tradebant ministrum etiam agere « in persona Ecclesiae », id est nomine totius Ecclesiae et ad eam repraesentandam. Re quidem vera, qualiscumque est, ad fideles quod attinet, participatio actionis liturgicae, totius tamen Ecclesiae nomine reapse celebrat sacerdos, quippe qui omnium nomine oret et in missa totius Ecclesiae sacrificium offerat: Ecclesia in novo Paschate Christum Dominum per sacerdotes sub

When the "fullness of time" (Gal 4:4) comes, the Word, the Son of God, takes on flesh in order to establish and seal the new and eternal covenant in his blood, which will be shed for many so that sins may be forgiven. His death will gather together again the scattered children of God; from his pierced side will be born the Church, as Eve was born from Adam's side.

At that time there is fully and eternally accomplished the nuptial mystery proclaimed and hymned in the Old Testament: Christ is the bridegroom; the Church is his bride, whom he loves because he has gained her by his blood and made her glorious, holy and without blemish, and henceforth he is inseparable from her.

This nuptial theme, which is developed from the Letters of St. Paul onwards (cf. 2 Cor 11:2; Eph 5:22-23) to the writings of St. John (cf. especially Jn 3:29; Rev 19:7, 9), is present also in the synoptic Gospels: the bridegroom's friends must not fast as long as he is with them (cf. Mk 2:19); the kingdom of heaven is like a king who gave a feast for his son's wedding (cf. Mt 22:1-14).

It is through this scriptural language, all interwoven with symbols and which expresses and affects man and woman in their profound identity, that there is revealed to us the mystery of God and Christ, a mystery which of itself is unfathomable.

That is why we can never ignore the fact that Christ is a man. And therefore, unless one is to disregard the importance of this symbolism for the economy of revelation, it must be admitted that, in actions which demand the character of ordination and in which Christ himself, the author of the covenant, the bridegroom and head of the Church, is represented, exercising his ministry of salvation—which is in the highest degree the case of the eucharist—his role (this is the original sense of the word *persona*) must be taken by a man. This does not stem from any personal superiority of the latter in the order of values, but only from a difference of fact on the level of functions and service.

Could one say that, since Christ is now in the heavenly condition, from now on it is a matter of indifference whether he be represented by a man or by a woman, since, "at the resurrection men and women do not marry" (Mt 22:30)? But this text does not mean that the distinc-

signis visibilibus immolat.[20] Cum ergo Ecclesiam quoque ipsam sacerdos repraesentet, num cogitari licet hanc congruenter cum supra descripta ratione signi a muliere posse repraesentari? Fatendum sane est sacerdotem reapse Ecclesiam repraesentare, quae est Corpus Christi; at hoc ideo, quia in primis Christum ipsum repraesentat, qui est caput et pastor Ecclesiae, quibus verbis Concilium Vaticanum II utitur, accuratius enuntians et complens locutionem *in persona Christi*.[21] Hoc munere fungens, sacerdos christianae synaxi praesidet atque eucharisticum sacrificium celebrat, in quo Ecclesia tota offert ipsaque offertur.[22]

Quicumque praedictis rationibus obsequi voluerit, melius intelleget, quam iustis de causis Ecclesia hoc modo se gesserit; ex iis denique controversiis, quae nostra aetate ortae sunt, utrum mulieres ordinationem recipere valeant necne, christiani incitari se sentiant, ut mysterium Ecclesiae · perscrutentur, naturam et significationem episcopatus et presbyteratus pressius investigent, item genuinum insignemque discernant locum sacerdotis in baptizatorum communitate, cuius membrum quidem est, a qua tamen secernitur, quia in iis actionibus, in quibus ordinationis character requiritur, sacerdos, cum illa efficacia, quae sacramentorum est propria, imago est ac signum ipsius Christi, qui convocat, absolvit, Foederis sacrificium conficit.

---

[20] Cf. Concilium Tridentinum, sessio 22, cap. 1: DS, n. 1741.

[21] Conc. Oec. Vat. II, Const. dogmat. *Lumen Gentium,* n. 28: *Munus Christi Pastoris et Capitis pro sua parte... exercentes;* Decret. *Presbyterorum Ordinis,* n. 2: *ita ut in persona Christi Capitis agere valeant...;* n. 6: munus Christi Capitis et Pastoris. – Cf Pius PP. XII, Litt. Enc. *Mediator Dei: altaris administer personam Christi utpote Capitis gerit, membrorum omnium nomine offerentis:* AAS 39 (1947), p. 556; – Synodus Episcoporum a. 1971, *De sacerdotio ministeriali,* I, 4: *Christum, Caput communitatis, praesentem reddit...*

[22] Paulus PP. VI, Litt. Enc. *Mysterium fidei,* 3 septembris 1965: A.S.S. 57 (1965), p. 761.

tion between man and woman, insofar as it determines the identity proper to the person, is suppressed in the glorified state; what holds for us holds also for Christ.

It is indeed evident that in human beings the difference of sex exercises an important influence, much deeper than, for example, ethnic differences: the latter do not affect the human person as intimately as the difference of sex, which is directly ordained both for the communion of persons and for the generation of human beings. In biblical revelation this difference is the effect of God's will from the beginning: "male and female he created them" (Gen 1:27).

However, it will perhaps be further objected that the priest, especially when he presides at the liturgical and sacramental functions, equally represents the Church: he acts in her name with "the intention of doing what she does." In this sense, the theologians of the Middle Ages said that the minister also acts *in persona Ecclesiae*, that is to say, in the name of the whole Church and in order to represent her. And in fact, leaving aside the question of the participation of the faithful in a liturgical action, it is indeed in the name of the whole Church that the action is celebrated by the priest: he prays in the name of all, and in the Mass he offers the sacrifice of the whole Church.

In the new Passover, the Church, under visible signs, immolates Christ through the ministry of the priest.[20] And so, it is asserted, since the priest also represents the Church, would it not be possible to think that this representation could be carried out by a woman, according to the symbolism already explained?

It is true that the priest represents the Church, which is the body of Christ. But if he does so, it is precisely because he first represents Christ himself, who is the head and shepherd of the Church. The Second Vatican Council[21] used this phrase to make more precise and to complete the expression *in persona Christi*. It is in this quality that the

---

[20] Cf. Council of Trent, Session 22, chap. 1: *DS* 1741

[21] Second Vatican Council, dogmatic constitution *Lumen Gentium*, 28: "Exercising within the limits of their authority the function of Christ as shepherd and head"; decree *Presbyterorum Ordinis*, 2: "that they can act in the person of Christ the head"; 6: "the office of Christ the head and the shepherd." Cf. Pope Pius XII, encyclical letter

VI. MINISTERIALE SACERDOTIUM
ECCLESIAE MYSTERIO ILLUSTRATUM

In memoriam vero opportune redigendum est quaestiones, quae oriantur e sacramentorum theologia et praesertim e sacerdotio ministeriali, de quo nunc agitur, solvi non posse nisi Revelationis luce affulgente. In iis enim solvendis humanae scientiae, quamvis magni sit aestimanda, quam in proprio ambitu conferant, cognitio, sufficere non possunt, quippe quae non apprehendant res fidei, in quibus, quod proprie supernaturale est, istarum scientiarum competentis iudicii non sunt.

Sic advertendum est, quantum Ecclesia a ceteris societatibus differat, natura et structura sua plane singularis. In Ecclesia enim pastorale munus cum ordinis sacramento pro more conectitur; non est ergo mere regimen, quod conferri possit iis potestatis formis, quae in rebus publicis inveniuntur. Non confertur spontaneo hominum delectu, etsi quidem forte per modum electionis designatur, qui munus accipiat: nonnisi enim per Apostolorum successorum manus impositionem et orationem electio ut a Deo facta confirmatur atque Spiritus Sanctus, qui in ordinatione datur, aliquem participem reddit regiminis Christi, supremi pastoris (cf *Act* 20,28). Quod munus est opus servitutis et amoris: *Si diligis me, pasce oves meas* (cf *Io* 21,15-17).

Quapropter non patet, quomodo proponi possit mulierum ad sacerdotium accessus ob eam, quae hominibus agnoscitur, iurium aequabilitatem, quaeque etiam christianis contingit. Ad quod probandum, nonnumquam ut argumento utuntur verbis supra allatis Epistulae ad Galatas (3,28), quibus declaratur nullam esse iam in Christo distinctionem viri et mulieris. His tamen verbis non agitur de ministeriis Ecclesiae, sed tantum asseritur omnes aequaliter vocari, ut adoptionem filiorum Dei accipiant. Praeterea ac potissimum, in ipsa ministerialis sacerdotii natura vehementer erraret, qui illud inter humana iura ascriberet, cum baptismus nemini ullum ius conferat ad publicum ministerium in Ecclesia adipiscendum. Sacerdotium enim alicui confertur, non ut ei honori sit vel commodo, sed ut Deo et Ecclesiae serviat; immo respondet vocationi peculiari et omnino gratuitae: *Non vos me elegistis, sed ego elegi vos et posui vos* (*Io* 15,16; cf *Heb* 5,4).

priest presides over the Christian assembly and celebrates the eucharistic sacrifice "in which the whole Church offers and is herself wholly offered."[22]

If one does justice to these reflections, one will better understand how well-founded is the basis of the Church's practice; and one will conclude that the controversies raised in our days over the ordination of women are for all Christians a pressing invitation to meditate on the mystery of the Church, to study in greater detail the meaning of the episcopate and the priesthood, and to rediscover the real and preeminent place of the priest in the community of the baptized, of which he indeed forms part but from which he is distinguished because, in the actions that call for the character of ordination, for the community he is—with all the effectiveness proper to the sacraments—the image and symbol of Christ himself who calls, forgives, and accomplishes the sacrifice of the covenant.

VI. THE MINISTERIAL PRIESTHOOD IN THE MYSTERY OF THE CHURCH

It is opportune to recall that problems of sacramental theology, especially when they concern the ministerial priesthood, as is the case here, cannot be solved except in the light of revelation. The human sciences, however valuable their contribution in their own domain, cannot suffice here, for they cannot grasp the realities of faith: the properly supernatural content of these realities is beyond their competence.

Thus one must note the extent to which the Church is a society different from other societies, original in her nature and in her structures. The pastoral charge in the Church is normally linked to the sacrament of order: it is not a simple government, comparable to the modes of authority found in states. It is not granted by people's spontaneous

Mediator Dei: "the minister of the altar represents the person of Christ as the head, offering in the name of all his members": _AAS_ 39 (1947), p. 556; 1971 Synod of Bishops, _De Sacerdotio Ministeriali_, I, 4: "(The priestly ministry) . . . makes Christ, the head of the community, present. . . ." .

[22] Pope Paul VI, encyclical letter _Mysterium Fidei_, September 3, 1965: _AAS_ 57 (1965), p. 761.

Dicunt interdum, vel in libris seu ephemeridibus passim scribunt, esse mulieres, quae in animo vocationem ad sacerdotium percipiant. Huiusmodi proclivitas, quamvis generosus et intellectu sit facilis, ad genuinam vocationem non sufficit: haec enim redigi nequit ad meram mentis inclinationem, quae subiectiva tantum maneret. Cum enim sacerdotium peculiare ministerium sit, cuius Ecclesia officium et custodiam acceperit, pro vocatione ad illud Ecclesiae auctoritas atque fides adeo expetenda est, ut eius sit pars constitutiva, nam Christus elegit *quos voluit ipse* (*Mc* 3,13). Rursus universalis est vocatio omnium baptizatorum ad regale sacerdotium exercendum, suam Deo offerendo vitam, atque testimonium reddendo in laudem Dei.

Mulieres, quae ministeriale sacerdotium se ambire profitentur, serviendi Christo Ecclesiaeque desiderio sane impelluntur. Nec mirum est quod, simul ac ipsae consciae fiunt olim discrimina se passas esse in civitate, ad id adducuntur, ut ipsum ministeriale sacerdotium sibi exoptent. Praetermittendum tamen non est sacerdotalem ordinem in humanae personae iuribus non contineri, sed e mysterii Christi et Ecclesiae oeconomia pendere. Presbyteri munus ambiri non potest quasi provectionem secum ferat in excelsiorem societatis dignitatem; nullus enim mere humanus sive societatis sive personae progressus ex sese capax est ad illud aditum praebendi, quippe cuius status omnino diversus sit.

Restat ergo, ut profundius meditemur inter maxima christianae professionis asserta genuinam illam baptizatorum aequabilitatem, quae ideo non est uniformitas, quia Ecclesia est corpus varietate membrorum distinctum, in quo suum cuique membro munus assignatur. Munera ergo distinguenda, non permiscenda sunt, nulli alterius in alterum exsuperantiae favent, aemulationis nomen non praebent. Unum charisma melius, quod quis aemulari potest ac debet, est caritas (cf *1 Cor* 12-13). Maiores in Regno caelorum non sunt ministri, sed sancti.

Exoptat sancta Mater Ecclesia, ut christianae mulieres sibi plene consciae fiant, quanta sit ipsarum missio: partes earum hodie maximae sunt, ut simul et instauretur atque humanior fiat societas et fideles veram Ecclesiae imaginem agnoscant.

choice: even when it involves designation through election, it is the laying on of hands and the prayer of the successors of the apostles that guarantee God's choice; and it is the Holy Spirit, given by ordination, who grants participation in the ruling power of the supreme pastor, Christ (cf. Acts 20:28). It is a charge of service and love: "If you love me, feed my sheep" (cf. Jn 21:15-17).

For this reason one cannot see how it is possible to propose the admission of women to the priesthood in virtue of the equality of rights of the human person, an equality which holds good also for Christians. To this end use is sometimes made of the text quoted above, from the Letter to the Galatians (3:28), which says that in Christ there is no longer any distinction between men and women. But this passage does not concern ministries: it only affirms the universal calling to divine filiation, which is the same for all.

Moreover, and above all, to consider the ministerial priesthood as a human right would be to misjudge its nature completely: baptism does not confer any personal title to public ministry in the Church. The priesthood is not conferred for the honor or advantage of the recipient, but for the service of God and the Church; it is the object of a specific and totally gratuitous vocation: "You did not choose me, no, I chose you; and I commissioned you. . ." (Jn 15:16; cf. Heb 5:4).

It is sometimes said and written in books and periodicals that some women feel that they have a vocation to the priesthood. Such an attraction, however noble and understandable, still does not suffice for a genuine vocation. In fact a vocation cannot be reduced to a mere personal attraction, which can remain purely subjective.

Since the priesthood is a particular ministry of which the Church has received the charge and the control, authentication by the Church is indispensable here and is a constitutive part of the vocation: Christ chose "those he wanted" (Mk 3:13). On the other hand, there is a universal vocation of all the baptized to the exercise of the royal priesthood by offering their lives to God and by giving witness for his praise.

Women who express a desire for the ministerial priesthood are doubtless motivated by the desire to serve Christ and the Church. And

Declarationem hanc Summus Pontifex Paulus divina Providentia PP. VI in Audientia concessa infrascripto Praefecto Sacrae Congregationis pro Doctrina Fidei, die 15 octobris a. 1976, ratam habuit, confirmavit atque evulgari iussit.

Datum Romae, ex Aedibus S. Congregationis pro Doctrina Fidei, die 15 mensis octobris 1976, in festo Sanctae Teresiae Abulensis.

FRANCISCUS Card. ŠEPER
Praefectus

✠ Fr. HIERONYMUS HAMER, O. P.
Archiepiscopus tit. Loriensis
Secretarius

it is not surprising that, at a time when they are becoming more aware of the discriminations to which they have been subject, they should desire the ministerial priesthood itself.

But it must not be forgotten that the priesthood does not form part of the rights of the individual, but stems from the economy of the mystery of Christ and the Church. The priestly office cannot become the goal of social advancement; no merely human progress of society or of the individual can of itself give access to it: it is of another order.

It therefore remains for us to meditate more deeply on the nature of the real equality of the baptized which is one of the great affirmations of Christianity: equality is in no way identity, for the Church is a differentiated body, in which each individual has his or her role. The roles are distinct, and must not be confused; they do not favor the superiority of some vis-a-vis the others, nor do they provide an excuse for jealousy; the only better gift, which can and must be desired, is love (cf. 1 Cor 12-13). The greatest in the kingdom of heaven are not the ministers but the saints.

The Church desires that Christian women should become fully aware of the greatness of their mission: today their role is of capital importance, both for the renewal and humanization of society and for the rediscovery by believers of the true face of the Church.

His Holiness Pope Paul VI, during the audience granted to the undersigned prefect of the Sacred Congregation on October 15, 1976 approved this declaration, confirmed it, and ordered its publication.

Given in Rome, at the Sacred Congregation for the Doctrine of the Faith, on October 15, 1976, the feast of St. Teresa of Avila.

✠ Cardinal Francis Seper
Prefect

✠ Jerome Hamer, OP
Secretary

A COMMENTARY ON THE DECLARATION
(Prepared by an Expert Theologian at the Request of the
Congregation for the Doctrine of the Faith)

Circumstances and Origins of the Declaration

The question of the admission of women to the ministerial priesthood seems to have arisen in a general way about 1958, after the decision by the Swedish Lutheran Church in September of that year to admit women to the pastoral office. This caused a sensation and occasioned numerous commentaries.

Even for the communities stemming from the sixteenth century Reformation it was an innovation: one may recall, for example, how strongly the *Confessio Fidei Scotiae* of 1560 accused the Roman Church of making improper concessions to women in the field of ministry. But the Swedish initiative gradually gained ground among the Reformed Churches, particularly in France, where various national synods adopted similar decisions.

In reality, the admission of women to the pastoral office seemed to raise no strictly theological problem, in that these communities had rejected the sacrament of order at the time of their separation from the Roman Church.

But a new and much more serious situation was created when ordinations of women were carried out within communities that considered that they preserved the apostolic succession of order: in 1971 and 1973 the Anglican bishop of Hong Kong ordained three women with the agreement of his synod; in July 1974 at Philadelphia there was the ordination in the Episcopal Church of eleven women—an ordination afterwards declared invalid by the House of Bishops.

Later on, in June 1975, the General Synod of the Anglican Church in Canada, meeting in Quebec, approved the principle of the accession of women to the priesthood; and this was followed in July by the General Synod of the Church of England: Dr. Coggan, Archbishop of Canterbury, frankly informed Pope Paul VI "of the slow but steady growth of a consensus of opinion within the Anglican Communion that there are no fundamental objections in principle to the ordination of women to the priesthood."

These are only general principles, but they might quickly be followed by practice, and this would bring a new and serious element into the dialogue with the Roman Catholic Church on the nature of the ministry. It has provoked a warning, first by the archbishop for the Orthodox in Great Britain, Athenagoras of Thyateira, and then, more recently, by Pope Paul VI himself in two letters to the Archbishop of Canterbury.

Furthermore, the ecumenical sectors brought the question to the notice of all the Christian denominations, forcing them to examine their positions of principle, especially on the occasion of the Assembly of the World Council of Churches at Nairobi in December 1975.

A completely different event has made the question even more topical: this was the organization under United Nations' auspices of International Women's Year in 1975. The Holy See took part in it with a Committee for International Women's Year, which included some members of the Commission for the Study of the Role of Women in Society and the Church, which had already been set up in 1973.

Ensuring respect for and fostering the respective rights and duties of men and women leads to reflection on participation by women in the life of society on the one hand, and in the life and mission of the Church on the other. Now, the Second Vatican Council has already set forth the task: "Since in our times women have an ever more active share in the whole life of society, it is very important that they participate more widely also in the various fields of the Church's apostolate." How far can this participation go?

It is understandable that these questions have aroused even in Catholic quarters intense studies, indeed passionate ones: doctoral theses, articles in reviews, even pamphlets, propounding or refuting in turn the biblical, historical, and canonical data and appealing to the human sciences of sociology, psychology, and the history of institutions and customs.

Certain famous people have not hesitated to take sides boldly, judging that there was "no basic theological objection to the possibility of women priests." A number of groups have been formed with a view to upholding this claim, and they have sometimes done this with insistence, as did the conference held in Detroit (U.S.A.) in November 1975 under the title "Women in Future Priesthood Now: A Call for Action."

The magisterium has thus been obliged to intervene in a question being posed in so lively a fashion within the Catholic Church and having important implications from the ecumenical point of view.

Archbishop Bernardin of Cincinnati, president of the U.S. National Conference of Catholic Bishops, declared on October 7, 1975 that he found himself "obliged to restate the Church's teaching that women are not to be ordained to the priesthood"; church leaders, he said, should "not seem to encourage unreasonable hopes and expectations, even by their silence."

Pope Paul VI himself had already recalled the same teaching. He did so at first in parenthetical fashion, especially in his address on April 18, 1975 to the members of the Study Commission on the Role of Women in Society and in the Church and the Committee for the Celebration of International Women's Year: "Although women do not receive the call to the apostolate of the Twelve and therefore to the ordained ministries, they are nonetheless invited to follow Christ as disciples and co-workers. . . . We cannot change what our Lord did, nor his call to women."

Later he had to make an express pronouncement in his exchange of letters with Dr. Coggan, Archbishop of Canterbury: "Your Grace is of course well aware of the Catholic Church's position on this question. She holds that it is not admissible to ordain women to the priesthood, for very fundamental reasons."

It is at his order that the Sacred Congregation for the Doctrine of the Faith has examined the question in its entirety. The question has been complicated by the fact that on the one hand arguments adduced in the past in favor of the traditional teaching are scarcely defensible today, and on the other hand the reasons given by those who demand the ordination of women must be evaluated.

To avoid the rather negative character that must mark the conclusions of such a study, one could have thought of inserting it into a more general presentation of the question of the advancement of women.

But the time is not ripe for such a comprehensive exposition, because of the research and work in progress on all sides.

It was difficult to leave unanswered any longer a precise question that is being posed nearly everywhere and which is polarizing attention to the detriment of more urgent endeavors that should be fostered. In fact, apart from its nonacceptance of the ordination of women, the document points to positive matters: a deeper understanding of the Church's teaching and of the ministerial priesthood, a call to spiritual progress, an invitation to take on the urgent apostolic tasks of today.

The bishops, to whom the document is primarily addressed, have the mission of explaining it to their people with the pastoral feeling that is theirs and with the knowledge they have of the milieu in which they exercise their ministry.

The declaration begins by presenting the Church's teaching on the question. This in fact has to be the point of departure. We shall see later how necessary it is to follow faithfully the method of using *loci theologici*.

The Tradition

It is an undeniable fact, as the declaration notes, that the constant tradition of the Catholic Church has excluded women from the episcopate and the priesthood. So constant has it been that there has been no need for an intervention by a solemn decision of the magisterium.

"The same tradition," the document stresses, "has been faithfully safeguarded by the Churches of the East. Their unanimity on this point is all the more remarkable since in many other questions their discipline admits of a great diversity. At the present time these same Churches refuse to associate themselves with requests directed towards securing the accession of women to priestly ordination."

Only within some heretical sects of the early centuries, principally Gnostic ones, do we find attempts to have the priestly ministry exercised by women. It must be further noted that these are very sporadic occurrences and are moreover associated with rather questionable practices.

We know of them only through the severe disapproval with which they are noted by St. Irenaeus in his *Adversus Haereses*, Tertullian in *De*

Praescriptione Haereticorum, Firmilian of Caesarea in a letter to St. Cyprian, Origen in a commentary on the First Letter to the Corinthians, and especially by St. Ephiphanius in his *Panarion*.

How are we to interpret the constant and universal practice of the Church? A theologian is certain that what the Church does she can in fact do, since she has the assistance of the Holy Spirit. This is a classical argument found again and again in St. Thomas with regard to the sacraments.

But what the Church has never done—is this any proof that she cannot do it in the future? Does the negative fact thus noted indicate a norm, or is it to be explained by historical and by social and cultural circumstances? In the present case, is an explanation to be found in the position of women in ancient and medieval society and in a certain idea of male superiority stemming from that society's culture?

It is because of this transitory cultural element that some arguments adduced on this subject in the past are scarcely defensible today. The most famous is the one summarized by St. Thomas Aquinas: *quia mulier est in statu subiectionis*. In St. Thomas' thought, however, this assertion is not merely the expression of a philosophical concept, since he interprets it in the light of the accounts in the first chapters of Genesis and the teaching of the First Letter to Timothy (2:12-14).

A similar formula is found earlier in the *Decretum* of Gratian, but Gratian, who was quoting the Carolingian Capitularies and the false Decretals, was trying rather to justify with Old Testament prescriptions the prohibition—already formulated by the ancient Church—of women from entering the sanctuary and serving at the altar.

The polemical arguments of recent years have often recalled and commented on the texts that develop these arguments. They have also used them to accuse the fathers of the Church of misogyny. It is true that we find in the fathers' writings the undeniable influence of prejudices against women. But it must be carefully noted that these passages had very little influence on their pastoral activity, still less on their spiritual direction, as we can see by glancing through their correspondence that has come down to us.

Above all it would be a serious mistake to think that such considerations provide the only or the most decisive reasons against the ordination of women in the thought of the fathers, of the medieval writers, and of the theologians of the classical period. In the midst of and going beyond speculation, more and more clear expression was being given to the Church's awareness that in reserving priestly ordination and ministry to men she was obeying a tradition received from Christ and the apostles and by which she felt herself bound.

This is what had been expressed in the form of an apocryphal literature by the ancient documents of church discipline from Syria, such as the *Didascalia Apostelorum* (middle of the third century) and the apostolic constitutions (end of the fourth or beginning of the fifth century), and by the Egyptian collection of twenty pseudoapostolic canons that was included in the compilation of the Alexandrian *Synodos* and translated into many languages.

St. John Chrysostom, for his part, when commenting on chapter 21 of John, understood well that women's exclusion from the pastoral office entrusted to Peter was not based on any natural incapacity, since, as he remarks, "even the majority of men have been excluded by Jesus from this immense task."

From the moment that the teaching on the sacraments is systematically presented in the schools of theology and canon law, writers begin to deal *ex professo* with the nature and value of the tradition that reserved ordination to men. The canonists base their case on the principle formulated by Pope Innocent III in a letter of December 11, 1210, to the bishops of Palencia and Burgos, a letter that was included in the collection of Decretals: "Although the Blessed Virgin Mary was of higher dignity and excellence than all the apostles, it was to them, not her, that the Lord entrusted the keys of the kingdom of heaven." This text became a *locus communis* for the *glossatores*.

As for the theologians, the following are some significant texts: St. Bonaventure: "Our position is this: it is due not so much to a decision by the Church as to the fact that the sacrament of order is not for them. In this sacrament the person ordained is a sign of Christ the mediator."

Richard of Middleton, a Franciscan of the second half of the thirteenth century: "The reason is that the power of the sacraments comes from their institution. But Christ instituted this sacrament for conferral on men only, not women."

John Duns Scotus: "It must not be considered to have been determined by the Church. It comes from Christ. The Church would not have presumed to deprive the female sex, for no fault of its own, of an act that might licitly have pertained to it." Durandus of Saint-Pourcain: ". . . the male sex is of necessity for the sacrament. The principal cause of this is Christ's institution. . . . Christ ordained only men . . . not even his mother. . . . It must therefore be held that women cannot be ordained, because of Christ's institution."

So it is no surprise that until the modern period the theologians and canonists who dealt with the question have been almost unanimous in considering this exclusion as absolute and having a divine origin. The theological notes they apply to the affirmation vary from "theologically certain" (*theologice certa*) to, at times, "proximate to faith" (*fidei proxima*) or even "doctrine of the faith" (*doctrina fidei*). Apparently, then, until recent decades no theologian or canonist considered that it was a matter of a simple law of the Church.

In some writers of the Middle Ages however there was a certain hesitancy, reported by St. Bonaventure without adopting it himself and noted also by Joannes Teutonicus in his gloss on *Caus.* 27, q. 1, c. 23. This hesitancy stemmed from the knowledge that in the past there had been deaconesses: had they received true sacramental ordination? This problem has been brought up again very recently.

It was by no means unknown to the seventeenth and eighteenth century theologians, who had an excellent knowledge of the history of literature. In any case, it is a question that must be taken up fully by direct study of the texts, without preconceived ideas; hence the Sacred Congregation for the Doctrine of the Faith has judged that it should be kept for the future and not touched upon in the present document.

The Attitude of Christ

In the light of tradition, then, it seems that the essential reason moving the Church to call only men to the sacrament of order and to the strictly priestly ministry is her intention to remain faithful to the type of ordained ministry willed by the Lord Jesus Christ and carefully maintained by the apostles. It is therefore no surprise that in the controversy there has been a careful examination of the facts and texts of the New Testament, in which tradition has seen an example establishing a norm.

This brings us to a fundamental observation: we must not expect the New Testament *on its own* to resolve in a clear fashion the question of the possibility of women acceding to the priesthood, in the same way that it does not on its own enable us to give an account of certain sacraments, and especially of the structure of the sacrament of order.

Keeping to the sacred text alone and to the points of the history of Christian origins that can be obtained by analyzing that text by itself would be to go back four centuries and find oneself once more amid the controversies of the Reformation. We cannot omit the study of tradition: it is the Church that scrutinizes the Lord's thought by reading scripture, and it is the Church that gives witness to the correctness of its interpretation.

It is tradition that has unceasingly set forth as an expression of Christ's will the fact that he chose only men to form the group of the Twelve. There is no disputing this fact, but can it be proved with absolute certainty that it was a question of a deliberate decision by Christ?

It is understandable that the partisans of a change in discipline bring all their efforts to bear against the significance of this fact. In particular, they object that, if Christ did not bring women into the group of the Twelve, it was because the prejudices of his time did not allow him to: it would have been an imprudence that would have compromised his work irreparably.

However, it has to be recognized that Jesus did not shrink from other "imprudences," which did in fact stir up the hostility of his fellow citizens against him, especially his freedom with regard to the rabbinical interpretations of the Sabbath. With regard to women his attitude was a complete innovation: all the commentators recognize that he went against many prejudices, and the facts that are noted add up to an impressive total.

For this reason greater stress is laid today on another objection: if Jesus chose only men to form the group of the Twelve, it was because he intended them to be a symbol representing the ancestors of the tribes of Israel ("You who have followed me will also sit on Twelve thrones and judge the tribes of Israel": Mt 19:28; cf. Lk 22:30); and this special motive, it is added, obviously referred only to the Twelve and would be no proof that the apostolic ministry should thereafter always be reserved to men. It is not a convincing argument.

We may note in the first place how little importance was given to this symbolism: Mark and John do not mention it. And in Matthew and Luke this phrase of Jesus about the twelve tribes of Israel is not put in the context of the call of the Twelve (Mt 10:1-4) but at a relatively late stage of Jesus' public life, when the apostles have long since been given their "constitution": they have been called by Jesus, have worked with him and been sent on missions.

Furthermore, the symbolism of Mt 19:28 and Lk 22:30 is not as certain as is claimed: the number could designate simply the whole of Israel. Finally, these two texts deal only with a particular aspect of the mission of the Twelve: Jesus is promising them that they will take part in the eschatological judgment. Therefore the essential meaning of their being chosen is not to be sought in this symbolism but in the totality of the mission given them by Jesus: "he appointed twelve; they were to be his companions and to be sent out to preach" (Mk 3:14).

As Jesus before them, the Twelve were above all to preach the good news (Mk 3:14; 6:12). Their mission in Galilee (Mk 6:7-13) was to become the model of the universal mission (Mk 12:10; cf. Mt 28:16-20). Within the messianic people the Twelve represent Jesus. That is the real reason why it is fitting that the apostles should be men: they act in the name of Christ and must continue his work.

It has been described above how Pope Innocent III saw a witness to Christ's intentions in the fact that Christ did not communicate to his mother, in spite of her eminent dignity, the powers which he gave to the apostles.

This is one of the arguments most frequently repeated by tradition: from as early as the third century the fathers present Mary as the example of the will of Jesus in this matter. It is an argument still particularly dear to Eastern Christians today. Nevertheless it is vigorously rejected by all those who plead in favor of the ordination of women.

Mary's divine motherhood, the manner in which she was associated with the redeeming work of her Son, they say, put her in an altogether exceptional and unique position; and it would not even be fair to her to compare her with the apostles and to argue from the fact that she was not ranked among them.

In point of fact these assertions do have the advantage of making us understand that there are different functions within the Church: the equality of Christians is in harmony with the complementary nature of their tasks, and the sacramental ministry is not the only rank of greatness, nor is it necessarily the highest: it is a form of service of the kingdom. The Virgin Mary does not need the increase in "dignity" that was once attributed to her by the authors of those speculations on the priesthood of Mary that formed a deviant tendency which was soon discredited.

The Practice of the Apostles

The text of the declaration stresses the fact that, in spite of the privileged place Mary had in the upper room after the ascension, she was not designated for entry into the college of the Twelve at the time of the election of Matthias. The same holds for Mary Magdalene and the other women who nevertheless had been the first to bring news of the resurrection.

It is true that the Jewish mentality did not accord great value to the witness of women, as is shown by Jewish law. But one must also note that the Acts of the Apostles and the Letters of St. Paul stress the role of women in evangelization and in instructing individual converts.

The apostles were led to take a revolutionary decision when they had to go beyond the circle of a Jewish community and undertake the evangelization of the Gentiles. The break with Mosaic observances was not made without discord. Paul had no scruples about choosing one of his collaborators, Titus, from among the Gentile converts (Gal 2:3).

The most spectacular expression of the change that the good news made on the mentality of the first Christians is to be found precisely in the Letter of the Galatians: "For as many of you as were baptized into Christ have put on Christ. There is neither Jew nor Greek, there is neither slave nor free, there is neither male nor female; for you are all one in Christ Jesus" (Gal 3:27-28).

In spite of this, the apostles did not entrust to women the strictly apostolic ministry, although Hellenistic civilization did not have the same prejudices against them as did Judaism. It is rather a ministry which is of another order, as may perhaps also be gathered from Paul's vocabulary, which a difference seems to be implied "my fellow workers" (*synergoi mou*) and "God's fellow workers" (*Theou synergoi*).

It must be repeated that the texts of the New Testament, even on such important points as the sacraments, do not always give all the light that one would wish to find in them. Unless the value of unwritten traditions is admitted, it is sometimes difficult to discover in scripture entirely explicit indications of Christ's will. But in view of the attitude of Jesus and the practice of the apostles as seen in the Gospels, the Acts, and the letters, the Church has not held that she is authorized to admit women to priestly ordination.

Permanent Value of This Practice

It is the permanency of this negative decision that is objected to by those who would have the legitimacy of ordaining women admitted. These objections employ arguments of great variety.

The most classic ones seek a basis in historical circumstances. We have already seen what is to be thought of the view that Jesus' attitude was inspired solely by prudence, because he did not want to risk compromising his work by going against social prejudices. It is claimed that the same prudence was forced upon the apostles.

On this point too it is clear from the history of the apostolic period that there is no foundation for this explanation. However, in the case of the apostles, should one not take into account the way in which they themselves shared these prejudices? Thus St. Paul has been accused of misogyny and in his letters are found texts on the inferiority of women that are the subject of controversy among exegetes and theologians today.

It can be questioned whether two of Paul's most famous texts on women are authentic or should rather be seen as interpolations, perhaps even relatively late ones. The first is 1 Cor 14:34-35: "The women should keep silence in the churches. For they are not permitted to speak, but should be subordinate as even the law says." These two verses, apart from being missing in some important manuscripts and not being found quoted before the end of the second century, present stylistic peculiarities foreign to Paul. The other text is 1 Tim 2:11-14: "I do not allow a woman to teach or to exercise authority over men." The Pauline authenticity of this text is often questioned, although the arguments are weaker.

However, it is of little importance whether these texts are authentic or not: theologians have made abundant use of them to explain that women cannot receive either the power of magisterium or that of jurisdiction. It was especially the text of 1 Timothy that provided St. Thomas with the proof that woman is in a state of submission or service, since (as the text explains) woman was created after man and was the person first responsible for original sin.

But there are other Pauline texts of unquestioned authenticity that affirm that "the head of the woman is the man" (1 Cor 11:3; cf. 8-12; Eph 5:22, 24). It may be asked whether this view of man, which is in line with that of the books of the Old Testament, is not at the basis of Paul's conviction and the Church's tradition that women cannot receive the ministry.

Now this is a view that modern society rejects absolutely, and many present-day theologians would shrink from adopting it without qualifying it. We may note however that Paul does not take his stand on a philosophical level but on that of biblical history: when he describes, in relation to marriage, the symbolism of love, he does not see man's superiority as domination but as a gift demanding sacrifice, in the image of Christ.

On the other hand there are prescriptions in Paul's writings that are unanimously admitted to have been transitory, such as the obligation he imposed on women to wear a veil (1 Cor 11:2-16). It is true that these are obviously disciplinary practices of minor importance, perhaps inspired by the customs of the time. But then there arises the more basic question: since the Church has later been able to abandon prescriptions contained in the New Testament, why should it not be the same with the exclusion of women from ordination?

Here we meet once again the essential principle that it is the Church herself that, in the different sectors of her life, ensures discernment between what can change and what must remain immutable. As the declaration specifies, "When she judges that she cannot accept certain changes, it is because she knows that she is bound by Christ's manner of acting. Her attitude, despite appearances, is therefore not one of archaism but of fidelity: it can be truly understood only in this light. The Church makes pronouncements in virtue of the Lord's promise and the presence of the Holy Spirit, in order to proclaim better the mystery of Christ and to safeguard and manifest the whole of its rich content."

Many of the questions confronting the Church as a result of the numerous arguments put forward in favor of the ordination of women must be considered in the light of this principle. An example is the following question dealt with by the declaration: why will the Church not change her discipline, since she is aware of having a certain power over the sacraments, even though they were instituted by Christ, in order to determine the sign or to fix the conditions for their administration? This faculty remains limited, as was recalled by Pius XII, echoing the Council of Trent: the Church has no power over the substance of the sacraments. It is the Church herself that must distinguish what forms part of the "substance of the sacraments" and what she can determine or modify if circumstances should so suggest.

On this point, furthermore, we must remember, as the declaration reminds us, that the sacraments and the Church herself are closely tied to history, since Christianity is the result of an event: the coming of the Son of God into time and to a country, and his death on the cross under

Pontius Pilate outside the walls of Jerusalem. The sacraments are a memorial of saving events. For this reason their signs are linked to those very events. They are relative to one civilization, one culture, although destined to be reproduced everywhere until the end of time.

Hence historical choices have taken place by which the Church is bound, even if speaking absolutely and on a speculative level other choices could be imagined. This, for instance, is the case with bread and wine as matter for the eucharist, for the Mass is not just a fraternal meal but the renewal of the Lord's supper and the memorial of his passion and thus linked with something done in history.

It has likewise been remarked that in the course of time the Church has agreed to confer on women certain truly ministerial functions that antiquity refused to give them in the very name of the example and will of Christ. The functions spoken of are above all the administration of baptism, teaching, and certain forms of ecclesiastical jurisdiction. As regards baptism, however, not even deaconesses in the Syriac-speaking East were permitted to administer it, and its solemn administration is still a hierarchical act reserved to bishop, priest, and, in accessory fashion, deacon. When urgently required, baptism can be conferred not only by Christians but even by unbaptized people whether men or women.

Its validity therefore does not require the baptismal character, still less that of ordination. This point is affirmed by practice and by theologians. It is an example of this necessary discernment in the Church's teaching and practice, a discernment whose only guarantee is the Church herself.

As regards teaching, a classical distinction has to be made, from Paul's letters onwards. There are forms of teaching or edification that lay people can carry out and in this case St. Paul expressly mentions women. These forms include the charisms of "prophecy" (1 Cor 11:15).

In this sense there was no obstacle to giving the title of doctor to Teresa of Avila and Catherine of Siena, as it was given to illustrious teachers such as Albert the Great or St. Laurence of Brindisi. Quite a different matter is the official and hierarchical function of teaching the revealed message, a function that presupposes the mission received from Christ by the apostles and transmitted by them to their successors.

Examples of participation by women in ecclesiastical jurisdiction are found in the Middle Ages: some abbesses (not abbesses in general, as is sometimes said in popularizing articles) performed acts normally reserved to bishops, such as the nomination of parish priests or confessors. These customs have been more or less reproved by the Holy See at different periods: the letter of Pope Innocent III quoted earlier was intended as a reprimand to the Abbess of Las Huelgas.

But we must not forget that feudal lords arrogated to themselves similar rights. Canonists also admitted the possibility of separating jurisdiction from order. The Second Vatican Council has tried to determine better the relationship between the two; the Council's doctrinal vision will doubtless have effects on discipline.

In a more general way, attempts are being made, especially in Anglican circles, to broaden the debate in the following way: is the Church perhaps bound to scripture and tradition as an absolute, when the Church is a people making its pilgrim way and should listen to what the Spirit is saying? Or else a distinction is made between essential points on which unanimity is needed and questions of discipline admitting of diversity: and if the conclusion reached is that the ordination of women belongs to those secondary matters, it would not harm progress towards the union of the Churches.

Here again it is the Church that decides by her practice and magisterium what requires unanimity, and distinguishes it from acceptable or desirable pluralism. The question of the ordination of women impinges too directly on the nature of the ministerial priesthood for one to agree that it should be resolved within the framework of legitimate pluralism between Churches. That is the whole meaning of the letter of Pope Paul VI to the Archbishop of Canterbury.

The Ministerial Priesthood in the Light of the Mystery of Christ

In the declaration a very clear distinction will be seen between the document's affirmation of the datum (the teaching it proposes with authority in the preceding paragraphs) and the theological reflection that then follows. By this reflection the Sacred Congregation for the Doctrine of the Faith endeavors "to illustrate this norm by showing the profound fittingness" to be found "between the proper nature of the sacrament of order, with its specific reference to the mystery of Christ, and the fact that only men have been called to receive priestly ordination."

In itself such a quest is not without risk. However, it does not involve the magisterium. It is well known that in solemn teaching infallibility affects the doctrinal affirmation, not the arguments intended to explain it. Thus the doctrinal chapters of the Council of Trent contain certain processes of reasoning that today no longer seem to hold.

But this risk has never stopped the magisterium from endeavoring at all times to clarify doctrine by analogies of faith. Today especially, and more than ever, it is impossible to be content with making statements, with appealing to the intellectual docility of Christians: faith seeks understanding, and tries to distinguish the grounds for and the coherence of what it is taught.

We have already discarded a fair number of explanations given by medieval theologians. The defect common to these explanations is that they claimed to find their basis in an inferiority of women vis-a-vis men; they deduced from the teaching of scripture that woman was "in a state of submission," of subjection, and was incapable of exercising functions of government.

It is very enlightening to note that the communities springing from the Reformation which have had no difficulty in giving women access to the pastoral office are first and foremost those that have rejected the Catholic doctrine on the sacrament of order and profess that the pastor is only one baptized person among others, even if the charge given has been the object of a consecration.

The declaration therefore suggests that it is by analyzing the nature of order and its character that we will find the explanation of the exclusive call of men to the priesthood and episcopate. This analysis can be outlined in three propositions: (1) in administering the sacraments that demand the character of ordination the priest does not act in his own name (*in persona propria*), but in the person of Christ (*in persona Christi*);

(2) this formula, as understood by tradition, implies that the priest is a sign in the sense in which this term is understood in sacramental theology; (3) it is precisely because the priest is a sign of Christ the savior that he must be a man and not a woman.

That the priest performs the eucharist and reconciles sinners in the name and place of Christ is affirmed repeatedly by the magisterium and constantly taught by fathers and theologians. It would not appear to serve any useful purpose to give a multitude of quotations to show this. It is the totality of the priestly ministry that St. Paul says is exercised in the place of Christ: "We are acting as ambassadors on behalf of Christ, God, as it were, appealing through us"—in fact this text from 2 Corinthians has in mind the ministry of reconciliation (5:18-20)—"you have received me as an angel of God, even as Christ Jesus" (Gal 4:14).

Similarly St. Cyprian echoes St. Paul: "The priest truly acts in the place of Christ." But theological reflection and the Church's life have been led to distinguish the more or less close links between the various acts in the exercise of the ministry and the character of ordination and to specify which require this character for validity.

Saying "in the name and place of Christ" is not however enough to express completely the nature of the bond between the minister and Christ as understood by tradition. The formula *in persona Christi* in fact suggests a meaning that brings it close to the Greek expression *mimema Christou*. The word *persona* means a part played in the ancient theater, a part identified by a particular mask. The priest takes the part of Christ, lending him his voice and gestures.

St. Thomas expresses this concept exactly: "The priest enacts the image of Christ, in whose person and by whose power he pronounces the words of consecration." The priest is thus truly a *sign* in the sacramental sense of the word. It would be a very elementary view of the sacraments if the notion of sign were kept only for material elements.

Each sacrament fulfills the notion in a different way. The text of St. Bonaventure already mentioned affirms this very clearly: "the person ordained is a sign of Christ the mediator."

Although St. Thomas gave as the reason for excluding women the much discussed one of the state of subjection (*status subiectionis*), he nevertheless took as his starting point the principle that "sacramental signs represent what they signify by a natural resemblance," in other words the need for that "natural resemblance" between Christ and the person who is his sign. And, still on the same point, St. Thomas recalls: "Since a sacrament is a sign, what is done in the sacrament requires not only the reality but also a sign of the reality."

It would not accord with "natural resemblance," with that obvious "meaningfulness," if the memorial of the supper were to be carried out by a woman; for it is not just the recitation involving the gestures and words of Christ, but an action, and the sign is efficacious because Christ is present in the minister who consecrates the eucharist, as is taught by the Second Vatican Council, following the encyclical *Mediator Dei.*

It is understandable that those favoring the ordination of women have made various attempts to deny the value of this reasoning. It has obviously been impossible and even unnecessary for the declaration to consider in detail all the difficulties that could be raised in this regard. Some of them however are of interest in that they occasion a deeper theological understanding of traditional principles.

Let us look at the objection sometimes raised that it is ordination—the character—not maleness, that makes the priest Christ's representative. Obviously it is the character, received by ordination, that enables the priest to consecrate the eucharist and reconcile penitents. But the character is spiritual and invisible (*res et sacramentum*). On the level of the sign (*sacramentum tantum*) the priest must both have received the laying on of hands and take the part of Christ. It is here that St. Thomas and St. Bonaventure require that the sign should have natural meaningfulness.

In various fairly recent publications attempts have been made to reduce the importance of the formula *in persona Christi* by insisting rather on the formula *in persona Ecclesiae.* For it is another great principle of the theology of the sacraments and liturgy that the priest presides over the liturgy in the name of the Church, and must have the intention of "doing what the Church does."

Could one say that the priest does not represent Christ, because he first represents the Church by the fact of his ordination? The declaration's reply to this objection is that, quite on the contrary, the priest represents the Church precisely because he first represents Christ himself, who is the head and shepherd of the Church. It indicates several texts of the Second Vatican Council that clearly express this teaching.

Here there may well be in fact one of the crucial points of the question, one of the important aspects of the theology of the Church and the priesthood underlying the debate on the ordination of women. When the priest presides over the assembly, it is not the assembly that has chosen or designated him for this role. The Church is not a spontaneous gathering. As its name of *ecclesia* indicates, it is an assembly that is convoked. It is Christ who calls it together. He is the head of the Church, and the priest presides "in the person of Christ the head" (*in persona Christi capitis*).

That is why the declaration rightly concludes "that the controversies raised in our days over the ordination of women are for all Christians a pressing invitation to meditate on the mystery of the Church, to study in greater detail the meaning of the episcopate and the priesthood, and to rediscover the real and preeminent place of the priest in the community of the baptized, of which he indeed forms part but from which he is distinguished because, in the actions that call for the character of ordination, for the community he is—with all the effectiveness proper to the sacraments—the image and symbol of Christ himself who calls, forgives, and accomplishes the sacrifice of the covenant."

However, the objectors continue: it would indeed be important that Christ should be represented by a man if the maleness of Christ played an essential part in the economy of salvation. But, they say, one cannot accord gender a special place in the hypostatic union: what is essential is the human nature—no more—assumed by the word, not the incidental characteristics such as the sex or even the race which he assumed. If the Church admits that men of all races can validly represent Christ, why should she deny women this ability to represent him?

We must first of all reply, in the words of the declaration, that ethnic differences "do not affect the human person as intimately as the difference of sex." On this point biblical teaching agrees with modern psychology. The difference between the sexes however is something willed by God from the beginning, according to the account in Genesis (which is also quoted in the Gospel), and is directed both to communion between persons and to the begetting of human beings. And it must be affirmed first and foremost that the fact that Christ is a man and not a woman is neither incidental nor unimportant in relation to the economy of salvation.

In what sense? Not of course in the material sense, as has sometimes been suggested in polemics in order to discredit it, but because the whole economy of salvation has been revealed to us through essential symbols from which it cannot be separated, and without which we would be unable to understand God's design. Christ is the new Adam. God's covenant with men is presented in the Old Testament as a nuptial mystery, the definitive reality of which is Christ's sacrifice on the cross.

The declaration briefly presents the stages marking the progressive development of this biblical theme, the subject of many exegetical and theological studies. Christ is the bridegroom of the Church, whom he won for himself with his blood, and the salvation brought by him is the new covenant: by using this language, revelation shows why the incarnation took place according to the male gender, and makes it impossible to ignore this historical reality. For this reason, only a man can take the part of Christ, be a sign of his presence, in a word "represent" him (that is, be an effective sign of his presence) in the essential acts of the covenant.

Could one do without this biblical symbolism when transmitting the message, in contemplating the mystery and in liturgical life? To ask this, as has been done in certain recent studies, is to call into question the whole structure of revelation and to reject the value of scripture. It will be said, for example, that "in every period the ecclesial community appeals to the authority it has received from its founder in order to choose the images enabling it to receive God's revelation." This is perhaps to fail even more profoundly to appreciate the human value of the nuptial theme in the revelation of God's love.

The Ministerial Priesthood in the Mystery of the Church

It is also striking to note the extent to which the questions raised in the controversy over the ordination of women are bound up with a certain theology of the Church. We do not of course mean to dwell on the excessive formulas which nonetheless sometimes find a place in theological reviews. An example is the supposition that the primitive Church was based on the charisms possessed by both women and men. Another is the claim that "the Gospels also present women as ministers of unction." On the other hand, we have already come across the question of the pluralism that can be admitted in unity and seen what its limits are.

The proposal that women should be admitted to the priesthood because they have gained leadership in many fields of modern life today seems to ignore the fact that the Church is not a society like the rest. In the Church, authority or power is of a very different nature, linked as it normally is with the sacrament, as is underlined in the declaration. Disregard of this fact is indeed a temptation that has threatened ecclesiological research at all periods: every time that an attempt is made to solve the Church's problems by comparison with those of states, or to define the Church's structure by political categories, the inevitable result is an impasse.

The declaration also points out the defect in the argument that seeks to base the demand that the priesthood be conferred on women on the text Galatians 3:28, which states that in Christ there is no longer any distinction between man and woman. For St. Paul this is the effect of baptism. The baptismal catechesis of the fathers often stressed it. But absolute equality in baptismal life is quite a different thing from the structure of the ordained ministry. This latter is the object of a vocation within the Church, not a right inherent in the person.

A vocation within the Church does not consist solely or primarily in the fact that one manifests the desire for a mission or feels attracted by an inner compulsion. Even if this spontaneous step is made and even if one believes one has heard as it were a call in the depths of one's soul, the vocation is authentic only from the moment that it is authenticated by the external call of the Church. The Holy Office recalled this truth in its 1912 letter to the bishop of Aire to put an end to the Lahitton controversy. Christ chose "those he wanted" (Mk 3:13).

Since the ministerial priesthood is something to which the Lord calls expressly and gratuitously, it cannot be claimed as a right, any more by men than by women. Archbishop Bernardin's declaration of October 1975 contained the sound judgment: "It would be a mistake . . . to reduce the question of the ordination of women to one of injustice, as is done at times. It would be correct to do this only if ordination were a God-given right of every individual; only if somehow one's human potential could not be fulfilled without it. In fact, however, no one, male or female, can claim a 'right' to ordination. And, since the episcopal and priestly office is basically a ministry of service, ordination in no way 'completes' one's humanity."

The declaration of the Sacred Congregation for the Doctrine of the Faith ends by suggesting that efforts in two directions should be fostered, efforts from which the pastors and faithful of the Church would perhaps be distracted if this controversy over women's ordination were prolonged.

One direction is in the doctrinal and spiritual order: awareness of the diversity of roles in the Church, in which equality is not identity, should lead us—as St. Paul exhorts us—to strive after the one gift that can and should be striven after, namely love (1 Cor 12-13). "The greatest in the kingdom of heaven are not the ministers but the saints," says the declaration. This expression deserves to be taken as a motto.

The other direction for our efforts is in the apostolic and social order. We have a long way to go before people become fully aware of the greatness of women's mission in the Church and society, "both for the renewal and humanization of society and for the rediscovery by believers of the true countenance of the Church." Unfortunately we also still have a long way to go before all the inequalities of which women are still the victims are eliminated, not only in the field of public professional and intellectual life, but even within the family.

COMMENTARIES

THE ADVANCEMENT OF WOMEN ACCORDING TO THE CHURCH

RAIMONDO SPIAZZI, OP

The theological nature of the "Declaration on the Question of the Admission of Women to the Ministerial Priesthood," issued by the Sacred Congregation for the Doctrine of the Faith by order of the sovereign pontiff, does not exclude but presupposes and involves consideration of the contemporary socio-cultural context. Within this context the entry of women into all areas and all levels of public life is one of the characterizing phenomena. John XXIII recognized this, in fact, in a page of the encyclical *Pacem in Terris* (*AAS* 55, 1963, pp. 267-268), from which the new document starts.

This great innovation of our century, which matured gradually among the ideological and social ferments of the nineteenth century, has certainly brought about a change in living conditions, outlook, and behavior. This change has exercised a determinant influence on the relations between man and woman, on the conception, the constitution, and the life of the family, and on the organization of society, giving rise to new demands and creating problems unknown before.

Careful and responsible reflection on the new reality, on the part of the Church, prompted in her pastors and teachers certain reserves. And these reserves still hold good when faced with the excesses of feminist movements and the risks of easy illusions and confusion that could alter the meaning of things (that is, of femininity, of the family, and of society), with harmful consequences on the moral, civil, and religious plane. But it also led to a new ecclesial awareness of the role of woman and her rights and duties in regard to active and responsible participation in the life of the civil and ecclesial community.

The Magisterium of the Church and Women's New Problems

Pius XII particularly dedicated his attention and exercised his magisterium to clarify this crucial problem of contemporary society. He did this in the post-war period just when all the ideological and passionate charges that had accumulated in the hearts of human beings in decades of experiences, tensions, and struggles exploded in the political field.

It is enough to glance through the analytical index of his *Discorsi e Radiomessaggi* to realize how he insisted on this matter in his interventions. They were all characterized, certainly, by concern to safeguard the originality of woman's nature, and her specific functions and personal dignity, in the new condition of society. But they were also marked by recognition of the aspirations and possibilities opened to woman by the evolution of the last half century and by the call to active commitment both in social and political life and in the apostolate of the Church. These pages constitute—also on the point—a milestone in the development of the social and pastoral doctrine of the Church. They are still relevant today, even if so many new aspirations for woman's advancement have emerged in the last twenty years, in a situation of culture and work that is deeply changed.

In fact there has come to the fore more and more a central problem concerning woman's status, formulated, according to current fashion, in terms of *struggle of liberation*. It is the demand to be liberated from the institutionalized egoisms, as one could call them, which in certain places, classes, and environments lead to the subjugation and exploitation of women. Interest in this problem has become generalized, with the result that, on the one hand, demands for radical changes have emerged, sometimes giving rise to disorderly and demagogic demonstrations. On the other hand, a juridico-political evolution has emerged which has recognized women as having many rights and has offered them many possibilities of achievement on the civil plane.

Perhaps feminist irredentism has neglected the interior aspect of the problem. The liberation from psychisms, frustrations, and complexes, unleashed under strong pressure of propaganda exploiting the occasion, can lead to extreme aberrations, the effect and sign of a dreadful degradation, cultural even more than moral. In this direction it is painful, for example, to see women and especially girls being recruited and joining marches to demand at the top of their voices the new "rights": sexual freedom, free management of their own body, the faculty of freely having an abortion and at the expense of the state, etc. It is indeed a disheartening sight. Fortunately, it is a question of agitated and whipped up minorities, but still they represent a pathological phenomenon that must be taken into account and for which a remedy must be found, especially by creating conditions of social life in which another more fundamental problem of woman's advancement can be solved: that of her positive elevation on the cultural, civil, and spiritual planes. This inevitably involves also an adequate formation, corresponding to the requirements of femininity.

In the last few years the magisterium of the Church has pointed out several times the paths to take and the criteria to adopt—for woman's real advancement, beyond all those mystifications and blunders which end up by leading them to loss of their own authenticity and, all things considered, to new forms of slavery.

Paul VI's Interventions

Paul VI's interventions on this matter are countless. Mention should be made here particularly of the address delivered on December 6, 1976 to participants in the National Congress of the Italian Women's Centre (cf. *L'Osservatore Romano*, English-language edition, December 16, 1976). In it the pope stresses forcefully the principles according to which it is necessary to work for woman's advancement according to the model proposed by the Church.

This advancement, for Paul VI, is beyond dispute, just as it is certain that it is far from being implemented. "We are fully convinced," he declares, "that the participation of women at the various levels of social life must be not only recognized, but also fostered and above all warmly appreciated; and certainly there is still a long way to go in this direction." But as the Second Vatican Council taught, women ought "to play their part fully according to their own particular nature" (*Gaudium et Spes*, no. 60), which, the pope adds, must not be renounced.

From a biblical and Christian point of view, it is necessary to recognize in woman the same "image and likeness" of God (Gn 1:26, 27), which "she has in common with man and which makes her fully his equal"; but this image "is realized in her in a particular way, which differentiates woman from man, no more, however, than man is differentiated from woman: not in dignity of nature, but in diversity of functions." So Paul VI adds at once the wise warning that "it is necessary to beware of a cunning form of belittlement of woman's status, in which it is possible to fall today, by refusing to recognize those diversifying features stamped by nature on both human beings. It belongs on the contrary to the order of creation that woman should fulfill herself as a woman, certainly not in a competition of mutual oppression with man, but in harmonious and fruitful integration, based on respectful recognition of the roles peculiar to each. It is therefore highly desirable that in the various fields of social life in which she has her place, woman should bring that unmistakably human stamp of sensitiveness and solicitude, which is characteristic of her."

In the allocution to members of the "Study Commission on Woman's Functions in Society and in the Church" and to members of the "Committee for Women's International Year," on April 18, 1975, Paul VI had already spoken of the different riches and dynamisms characteristic of man and woman, which must lead to a world that is not leveled and uniform, but harmonious and unified (cf. *L'Osservatore Romano*, English-language edition, May 1, 1975). For the Church, therefore, the equality of the sexes is not identity. The juridical parity recognized in the most recent constitutions and legislations does not mean confusion of roles and cancellation of original characteristics. Advancement cannot have as its purpose oppression or the conquest of hegemony, but must aim at the harmonization of functions and implementation of the complementarity on the psychologico-affective, operational, spiritual, and structural plane (in the family and society). This, according to the Bible, is willed by the Creator. It is also obvious from an objective examination of the human reality of the two sexes.

With these indispensable clarifications and, where necessary, reserves in judgment on ideologies, laws, and methods of action of our times, the Church gives her full and sincere support and encouragement to all initiatives that wish to implement the justice often lacking in women's status. The pope says so, referring to the council: "The whole Church follows with great interest and trepidation the various women's movements which aim at reaching 'parity with men in fact as well as of rights' (*Gaudium et Spes*, no. 9). In Christianity, in fact, more than in any other religion, woman has had right from the beginning a special status of dignity. . . ." And after summing up the testimonies of the New Testament on the new importance given to women by Jesus, the apostles, and the first communities, the pope points out that from these texts "it is clearly evident that woman is given a place in the living and operating structure of Christianity, such an important place that perhaps all its virtualities have not yet been clarified. . . ." And here is the conclusion of great topical interest: "Like the Church of the origins, so also the Church of today cannot but be on the side of woman, especially where the latter, from being an active and responsible subject, is put in the humiliating position of a passive and insignificant object: as in certain environments of work and in certain of the lower forms of instrumentalization of the mass media, in social relations, and in the family. One would think that for some people woman represents today the easiest instrument to give expression to their tendencies to violence and tyranny. In this way the harsh attitude of some women's movements can be explained and, in part, understood. . . ."

"On the side of woman," therefore: for her liberation and true advancement; for overcoming discriminations contrary to God's plan, and in the first place discrimination based on sex (cf. *Gaudium et Spes*, no. 29): this is the position of the Church emphasized by Paul VI and recalled from the first page of the new declaration of the Sacred Congregation for the Doctrine of the Faith.

But at this point one may ask the question: if things are so, how can one explain the negative solution that the declaration itself gives to the question of woman's admission to the ministerial priesthood? What is the reasoning, in relation to the premises on liberation and advancement, that leads the declaration to conclude by reaffirming and strengthening discrimination based on the difference of sex?

Well, a dispassionate and calm reading of the declaration makes it possible to draw from the authentic sources of Catholic doctrine and discipline—that is, Holy Scripture and Christian tradition and practice going back to the apostles and to the first communities, and therefore to Jesus—the reasons for the attitude of the Church, never modified in two thousand years of historical experience. As will be explained in subsequent articles, the declaration connects these reasons with the mystery of God's eternal plan regarding the organization of the means of salvation in the economy of grace carried out in the world by Christ. But in clarifying this doctrine with theological reasons, albeit not demonstrative but connected with other certain points of revelation (analogy of faith), the document lists some arguments which—beyond the theological sphere of the question dealt with—can give strength and at the same time balance to the whole religious and civil project for the advancement of woman.

In the first place the value of a "sign," which is inherent in the sacraments, is extended to the person of the minister. It makes it possible to see in the priest the reflection of the image of Christ, who "was and remains a man." But it also makes it possible to connect the relationship between the man-priest and the community of the faithful in the logic of the union or covenant between God and mankind, which is presented in the Old and in the New Testament as a nuptial mystery. The man-priest, by virtue of his ordination, operates in the name, in the place of, and by virtue of Christ: *in persona Christi*, as St. Thomas says (cf. III, q. 83, a. 1, ad 3), and the council confirms (cf. *Sacrosanctum Concilium*, no. 33; *Lumen Gentium*, nos. 10, 28; *Presbyterorum Ordinis*, nos. 2, 13, etc.). The declaration clarifies and completes this traditional doctrine, explaining that it is a question of a reflection of Christ as "author of the covenant, bridegroom and head of the Church," the eternal Word who, to carry out God's plan historically, became incarnate in our human nature according to the male sex, certainly not to affirm a natural superiority of man over woman, but raising to the summit of creation—where the mystery of incarnation is placed—the duality, complementarity, and correlativity of the sexes.

The symbolism of this mystery, which pervades the historical fact of the existence of Jesus the man, in requiring that the priesthood should be conferred on persons of the male sex, does not mortify the figure of woman, but stresses, if anything, the importance of the sexual difference, which "in human beings . . . has an important influence, much deeper, for example, than ethnic differences: the latter do not affect the human person as intimately as the difference of sex, which is directly ordained both to the communion of persons and to the generation of human beings." This adds up to a reaffirmation of the intrisic value, the dignity, the relative autonomy, the originality of function, the necessity of intervention also of the female sex. This means that woman, in the bride-Church of which she bears the image in herself, and by extension of point of view and application of principles, also in the world, is worthy of respect and of advancement, as a woman and not according to other considerations.

This conclusion can be reached without straining the meaning, it seems to us, starting just from the thesis emphasized by the declaration.

Many Mansions in the Church

The document prompts another consideration. Before concluding, it points out that in the Church no one, either male or female, can claim the right to priestly ordination. This applies even when it is claimed on account of a deep feeling that one is called to the priesthood, or that one can reach the fullness of his character as a Christian, or even of his own human condition, only within the priesthood. Actually, the priesthood "is not part of the rights of the person," but is a gift and a power that is conferred by means of the Church on those whom the Church herself judges suitable—thus confirming the vocation with her objective judgment—according to the requirements of God's plan and Christ's institution.

But right from the beginning the declaration recalls and singles out for praise women who, as history shows, "have played a decisive role in the life of the Church and carried out tasks of considerable value." The declaration mentions the foundresses of great religious families, the outstanding teachers of doctrine and spiritual life, those who provided works of assistance and charity, the women apostles in mission countries, "as well as those Christian wives who exercised a deep influence on their families and, in particular, transmitted the faith to their children." It could be added that there is hardly a country, a community, in which there do not exist the signs of the incalculable benefits received from some of these outstanding of women: whether they be the great accomplishers of works of charity or apostolate, or humble, silent collaborators—sisters and lay women—of the Church and of the groups of which she is made up, in doing good in all its forms. Which of us does not remember some of these marvelous creatures, to whom perhaps we owe a lot of the good received and accumulated from childhood? Who does not meet them continually at every crossroads along the ways of the Church?

It can be deduced from this daily reality that there are "many mansions" in the Church and that there is room for a great wealth of ministries and charisms, without any need that they should be reduced, so to speak, to the priestly condition. The priesthood is one of many ministries. It implies a sacramental character of its own and charisms of its own, its own "professional graces," which are certainly of superior level. But it is not the only form or the only source of the apostolate. It is just this non-exclusiveness of the priesthood that emphasizes the greatness that can be reached by men and women outside the hierarchical line but always in the communion of the Church. This is proved by innumerable doers of good whom we can find in history. Already in the time of the apostolic communities so many noble figures of women apostles stand out. There are, for example, Priscilla, Lydia, Phoebe, recalled with gratitude and affection by St. Paul, and above all there is the Virgin Mary. And these figures remain throughout history right up to the Church of today, in which women are called to new roles at the level both of the parish and of the diocese, and even in various organisms of the Holy See, as the declaration recalls.

"The Greatest in the Kingdom of Heaven are the Saints"

This document, if read well—that is, seriously and serenely—can serve to give new impetus to the initiatives of the laity and especially of women in the apostolate, helping them all, and the latter particularly, to avoid the danger of "clericalization" that is latent under certain demands for the priesthood. It will be a question, for everyone, of recalling that the Virgin Mary, as Innocent III wrote, although superior in dignity and excellence to all the apostles, did not receive, like them, the keys of the kingdom (cf. *Corpus Iuris*, Decree: lib. 5, tit. 38, *De Poenit*, c. 10, Nova: quoted by the declaration). The late Cardinal Journet, when asked one day what he thought of the possible admission of women to the priesthood, replied simply as follows: "In the Church there is the greatness of hierarchy and the greatness of charity: the Blessed Virgin was placed at the summit of the latter greatness."

The Declaration of the Sacred Congregation for the Doctrine of the Faith also follows this line. After saying that "the Church is a differentiated body, in which each one has his function; the tasks are distinct and must not be confused. They do not give rise to the superiority of some over others; they do not furnish any pretext for jealousy; the only superior charism, which can and must be desired, is charity (cf. 1 Cor 12:12)," concludes with the following memorable words: "The greatest in the kingdom of heaven are not the ministers, but the saints."

This is the context of faith and spirituality that the Church considers the advancement of woman. For the Church the thread of the subject cannot but be this. But it may take us very far, as can be seen from the final wish of the declaration: "The Church desires that Christian women should become fully aware of the greatness of their mission: today their role is of capital importance, both for the renewal and humanization of society and for the rediscovery by believers of the true face of the Church." How could we renounce saying, at this point, that if the ministerial priesthood reflects the image of Christ, the head and bridegroom, the Christian woman is called to reflect in herself and reveal the identity of the bride-Church, the supreme figure and type of which is a woman whose name is Mary? The principle of the "eternal feminine" in Christianity did not clothe itself in myths, but became history in the Mary-Christ pair. The latter instills in the Church and expands all over the world the redeeming dynamism which aims at "making all things new" and especially at reestablishing in every man and every woman, as in new Adams and new Eves, participating in the "new life" of Christ and Mary, the original harmony of nature, noble, intact, and fresh, as it had come from God's hands.

SIGNIFICANCE FOR US TODAY OF CHRIST'S ATTITUDE AND OF THE PRACTICE OF THE APOSTLES

✠ ALBERT DESCAMPS

The recent declaration of the Sacred Congregation for the Doctrine of the Faith dedicates a large part to recalling the attitude of Christ (no. 2) and apostolic practice (no. 3), going on to show its permanent value (no. 4). In this article we recall in the first place this attitude and this practice, which are first of all historical facts; then we shall illustrate their valid significance for the Church today.

Attitude of Christ and Apostolic Practice

Jesus did not call any woman to join the group of the Twelve. This is a "material" fact, which does not need to be proved and which, as such, will not be questioned by anyone.

Of course, it is never enough to limit oneself to noting a material fact: it is also necessary to interpret it and understand it in depth. Today less than ever is the historical method content—the same applies also to the other human sciences—to record mere facts; it wishes above all to investigate their *meaning*. At present, what we wish to discover is the meaning given by Christ *himself* to the fact in question: this is first and foremost a problem that concerns the Christian historian and exegete. We will say further on what is the meaning of this fact *for us* today; this will be, if you like, a typical hermeneutical method in the sense that will be indicated.

To try to understand in depth the attitude of a personality of the past—in this case the fact that Jesus chose men as collaborators—means, in short, trying to discover what he *wanted* and to what extent he wanted it; it means studying his *intentions*.

In an investigation of this kind, the historical, let us admit, meets with new difficulties today. In general, traditional historiography was often in agreement with an anthropology of common sense, judged too simple today. This human person being defined by reason and will—*actus humani*, in opposition to mere *actus hominis*—it was tacitly supposed that he was fully responsible and free, and this all the more clearly when it was a question of remarkable personalities.

Contemporary anthropology dedicates more ample space to the concept of *conditioning*. Let us leave aside alleged determinisms of the unconscious type (studied by depth psychology) since some people propose in this case a *sociological* interpretation of the Gospel: choosing men as disciples, they tell us, Jesus was subject to the influence of cultural domination.

We grant that the traditional points of view generally tended to schematize too much the relations between individual and environment. According to these views, the human person is completely compact in himself—*in se compacta tota*—he can be isolated, he stands out clearly against the backdrop which is his environment. The latter, being only a "circumstance," refers to something exterior *(circumstare)*. Certainly, it has always been admitted that the individual can undergo the influences of his environment, but it was considered that they did not go beyond a certain level and that they could not jeopardize the full autonomy of the person. Today, on the contrary, this full autonomy is questioned, even in the case of Jesus. It is materially correct, some will say, that Jesus chose only men to make up the college of the Twelve. But, rather than a deeply reflective act, could not this be an attitude inspired by the environment? Did not the Master just conform to the customs of the time, and would he have acted in the same way in an environment that granted a more favorable position to women?

Such questions cannot be rejected *a priori,* even when it is a question of Jesus. Our faith in the divinity of the Savior does not prevent us from recognizing that, in his human psychology, Jesus may have been influenced, at least partly, by the environment in which he lived. This is one of the reasons why the life of Jesus can be studied by the historian first of all. The "truth" of the incarnation entails this tribute, as Charles

Péguy put it: "Jesus Christ put himself in the hands of the exegete, the historian, the critic, as he put himself in the hands of other judges, other multitudes. . . . If he had evaded criticism and controversy . . . if his memory had not entered the general conditions, the organic conditions of the memory of man, he would not have been a man like others at all. And the incarnation would not have been complete and true" (*Oeuvres en prose*, Gallimard, 1961, p. 1477).

We must not take up an *a priori* attitude against the influence of the environment, but it would be an even more regrettable prejudice to claim to dissolve the human person in the environment. Both before and after the recent developments of sociology, the historian generally finds himself in the presence of two great factors for the explanation of reality: the influence of the environment and the creative impact of personalities. The historian must continue to accept these two factors jointly and not as a dilemma: it is not a question "of environment *or* genius," but rather "of environment *and* genius." The essential thing is to examine each case objectively in the light of the historical documents. Today as in the past, it is necessary to emphasize, whenever the sources invite us to do so, the creative virtualities of the personalities of the past: their capacity of mastering the cultural environment, of really breaking with it and opening new ways; genius and creative freedom have not become empty words.

When it is a question of the origins of Christianity, the mere historian is already ready to recognize the originality of the person and action of Jesus, while the believer cannot but agree entirely with this. With Jean Guitton, it is permissible here to have recourse to the distinction between "spirit" and "mentality" (*Le problème de Jésus*, pp. 191-197). The spirit is the new, original contribution of a really original, creative individual; poured out right into the mentality, it questions, and it obliges it to change. And in the precise problem with which we are dealing, the evangelical documentation itself rightly shows us that Jesus established deep innovations with his attitude towards women.

To illustrate the attitudes of esteem and understanding that Jesus had towards women, the declaration recalls several passages from the

Gospel, known to every Christian. They are, for example, the texts that recall Jesus' attitude towards the Samaritan woman, the sinful woman, and the adulteress, and those that mention the women who accompany the Master in his itinerant ministry or who bring the paschal message to the Twelve. We have here at least "a set of converging indications." The Savior does not share, therefore, the prejudices of his contemporaries against women. Jesus' stand "contrasts exceptionally with that of his environment and marks a deliberate and courageous break."

Yet Jesus did not call any woman to take part directly in his Messianic mission; even Mary, "whose unequaled role is emphasized by the Gospels of Luke and John, was not invested with the apostolic ministry."

The conclusion is clear and inevitable: if Jesus did not take women as his direct collaborators, while in other ways he shows such benevolence towards then, it was not because of a concession, conscious or not, to a certain prevailing anti-feminism, or out of a kind of absent-minded conformism with the customs of his time.

The document of the Sacred Congregation for the Doctrine of the Faith keeps to this essential consideration: on associating only men closely in his work, Jesus did not act in this way to accommodate himself to the "male" mentality of his age. We think, however, that we are remaining faithful to the spirit of the declaration if we add here two reflections: one on the specificity of the concept of apostle, the other on its importance.

Jesus surrounds himself with apostles; however familiar it is to us, this image is seen, however, to be completely original as soon as we try to find models of it in the surrounding world or in biblical tradition. Some distant analogies can be found in the "disciples" of the prophets or of John the Baptist, or in the "pupils" of the doctors of the law; reference has also been made to the Jewish institution of "sending on a mission." But everything considered—it would take too long to show it here in detail—the institution of the Twelve appears as exceptionally original.

Another reflection is that it is a question here of a fundamental initiative in Jesus' thought. However far back we go in his public life, it does not seem that the Master ever exercised the ministry *alone:* in fact he chose his first disciples immediately after his baptism; the term "disciple" is to be taken here in a precise "ministerial" sense (Mk 1:16ff and parallel passages, Jn 1:35ff). Jesus alone in front of the multitudes: this is an image that is hardly used in the Gospels. Jesus apparently considers the help of his apostles necessary even during his mortal life to carry out God's plan. How much more does he feel the necessity of this assistance after his death, when the apostles, from being companions in work, will become his heirs, charged with continuing in the Church the construction of the kingdom of God.

The argumentation can be developed as follows: if Jesus is seen to be so highly *original* in organizing the group of the Messianic community in this way, and if the apostolic ministry takes on such great *importance* in his eyes, how is it possible to suppose that the Savior did not choose his apostles in a particularly deliberate way? How is it possible to suppose that he chose men only out of mere conformism? One Gospel text is particularly significant in this connection: Jesus chose "those whom he desired" (Mk 3:13).

In conclusion, instead of being what some people would be tempted to call an *obiter factum,* the fact that Jesus chose only men as direct associates reveals a sufficiently precise plan. The Master had remained free enough with regard to accepted ideas to entrust the preaching of the kingdom to women, if this had been his will and if he had considered this initiative to be part of God's plan.

What we have just said can be completed briefly by recalling the practice of the apostles *(Declaration,* no. 3). Right from the beginning of apostolic history, two men are the candidates for the election that must complete the college of the Twelve, in spite of the fact that Mary occupied a privileged place in a group that met in the Upper Room (Acts 1:14). In the writings of the New Testament as a whole, we can speak of a kind of contrast: on the one hand, complete silence regarding the official and public proclamation of the message by women, on the other hand allusions to help given in various ways by Christians to the preachers of the Gospel: Acts 18:26; Rom 16:1, 3-12; Phil 4:2-3, etc.

The silence in question is not fortuitous, but significant. And the "freedom" with which the apostles ask women to help them proves that they feel freed, following the example of Jesus, from the rigid prescriptions of Mosaicism; it is also possible that Christian missionaries were open to what some historians call a certain movement in favor of the advancement of women in the Greco-Roman world. If, however, the question did not arise of conferring the priesthood on women, this was not because of attachment to cultural "influences," but certainly out of faithfulness to Jesus of Nazareth.

Significance of These Facts for the Present Day

To seek the overall meaning of the behavior and intentions of Jesus or of the apostles, we must first find these attitudes or intentions, since they belong to the past; and this is what we have just done. But another step has also to be taken: we must ask ourselves what is the significance of these facts of other times *for us, today.* Moreover, it is this very meaning that the term "hermeneutics" tends to assume in our days: not only interpretation of the Scripture by the believer interested in a certain past, but also the search for the *permanent* value of the result of historical and Christian exegesis. The question is therefore the following: are the actions and the choices of Jesus and the apostles still normative *quoad nos?* In the declaration, this is a question that forms the object of a separate exposition (no. 4).

Among those who put forward the possibility of innovations in this matter, some affirm or suggest, as we have said, that the Master and his disciples simply could not "dream" of associating women in their work as ministers of the word, for the reason that the environment was not favorable. Choosing men as collaborators, Jesus and the apostles did not therefore display their firmest intentions.

If this had really been the case with regard to their intentions, it would certainly be unlikely that they should continue to be imposed today. Rather, the idea of their permanent value would be undermined at the foundations, and it is for this reason that the declaration (no. 4) begins by refuting this objection. It does so by summing up what it had proved before: "examination of the Gospels . . . shows . . . that Jesus broke with the prejudices of his time, ignoring to a large extent the discriminations practiced with regard to women. It cannot be sustained, therefore, that, in not calling any woman to enter the apostolic group, Jesus was guided only by reasons of expediency. With all the more reason, this socio-cultural conditioning would not have held back the apostles in the Greek environment, where the same discriminations did not exist."

Others formulate the following objection: is it not quite clear that Paul, in connection with woman, issued prescriptions deeply marked by the customs of the times, such as the obligation for a woman to wear a veil on her head (1 Cor 11:2-16)? Do we not lay our finger here on the socio-cultural, and therefore outdated, conditioning of some apostolic precepts? Could not this consideration be extended to other injunctions of the apostles, or even to some stands taken by Jesus himself?

The answer of the Sacred Congregation for the Doctrine of the Faith is inspired by the following principle: in this matter, the best thing is to examine each case presented separately, while it would be dangerous to express a uniform "value judgment." The requirement of the veil for women is not of great importance and, in any hypothesis, it has merely a disciplinary character. On the contrary, the prohibition for women to "speak" in Church (1 Cor 14:34-35; 1 Tm 2:12) is of another nature. For the apostle, woman has the right to prophesy at Christian meetings (1 Cor 11:5, etc.), but not to give official teaching. In his eyes, it is a question of a prescription connected with the divine plan of creation (1 Cor 11:7; Gn 2:18-24). But, once more, there is no point in accusing Paul of hostile preconceptions with regard to women: it is to him, on the contrary, that we owe "one of the most forceful texts in the New Testament on the fundamental equality of man and woman, as children of God in Christ" (cf. Gal 3:28). Furthermore, the apostle's confidence in women is well known, since he calls upon them to collaborate in many forms of his apostolate.

Another argument put forward by the supporters of an evolution in this matter is the idea, widely admitted by theology and the magisterium, that the Church has very vast powers with regard to the sacraments. That is true, we admit with the declaration, but it is a question of a limited power. The Council of Trent says so clearly in a well-known formula *(salva eorum substantia);* Pius XII repeated it, clarifying that this "substance" to be safeguarded concerns "everything that Christ the Lord, according to the testimony of the sources of Revelation, wished to be maintained in the sacramental sign."

To say that this continuity is necessary also means understanding that the sacramental signs are not conventional. Not only do they correspond to the deep symbolism of acts and things, but they also connect the man of all time with *the* event of the history of salvation, by means of all the riches of the pedagogy and symbolism of the Bible. "Adaptation to civilizations and historical periods cannot abolish, therefore, on essential points, the sacramental reference to the fundamental events of Christianity and to Christ himself." In the last analysis, it is the Church, by means of the voice of her magisterium, which "ensures discernment between what can change and what must remain immutable."

In a word: the example of Christ and the practice of the apostles maintain, in our case, a normative character; the Church is right to consider the fact of conferring priestly ordination only on men as in conformity with God's plan.

In addition to the objections already met, there is perhaps one of a more radical character, examination of which will make it possible to formulate an absolutely fundamental principle.

Let us admit, some people will say, that Jesus and his apostles clearly intended that their immediate collaborators should be men. Does it follow, they object, that these intentions have an imprescriptible value for Christians of all times? Is the Church bound to the Scriptures and to tradition as to an absolute, when she is, on the contrary, a pilgrim people, listening to what the Spirit says?

To answer adequately the question formulated in this way, it seems to us necessary to take seriously the fact that God's plan was realized in a quite peculiar way in biblical times. It is not sufficient to say that this plan was revealed, in the strict sense, in a given historical period; it must be added that it is marked by it forever. The divine plan is not a set of abstract ideas, but a work set in time and unfolded by a word that is deeply rooted in it. Prepared in the events and in the message of the Old Testament, this work and this word reached their climax in Jesus Christ, who is himself Event and Word: in his incarnation, his earthly ministry, his death and resurrection. Jesus' work and word are further prolonged at a privileged level in the apostolic Church: the apostles are historically the nearest interpreters of Christ's acts, and theologically the most authoritative commentators; from the second century, the Church is aware that the New Testament is complete and that the revelation was closed with the apostles.

If this is so, the *gesta Dei* illustrated by the two testaments were not only a starting signal, in relation to subsequent history. Nor were they merely a set of precise events commented on by contingent words. The public revelation was not the mere starting point of a growth and of an ideology such as could be incessantly remodeled in all freedom according to the changing vicissitudes of human history. Event and Word were founding facts, not only because they triggered off a given process, but also for the reason that they remain efficacious in that they are present and active in what the Church does: both by presenting the word in an up-to-date form without corrupting it, and by reproducing Christ's salvific act in the eucharist and, *proportione servata,* in the other sacraments. Certainly, the Church has the obligation to make herself understood by every generation and therefore to "translate" and update what it brings them; but she is also the bearer of realities, which must also "inform" in the etymological sense of the word, that is, model, mark with their seal the very tissue of history. To update does not mean to recreate freely: it is the same past that must become relevant today, on pain of being dissolved in time and of bringing about a crisis of identity in Christianity itself.

Therefore, when, on some important points of the economy of the kingdom of God, we perceive forms of behavior and deliberate intentions of Jesus or the apostles, interpreted in a constant way for nineteen centuries, it would be fatal not to recognize them as having a lasting value. A precise example of these important points is the choice of male collaborators by Jesus and the apostles.

Christianity is a historical religion at different levels, but above all in the sense that its origins were not only a starting point, but had a *content* which, in the essential points, marks it forever. The Church, therefore, must always refer to her beginnings. She does so certainly also by seeking dialogue with the present world, while her sense of the past is not precisely at the archeological level. But deep faithfulness to the origins is neither servility or sclerosis; it is rather a real guarantee of fruitfulness, since the origins themselves had a character of fullness; it was a question of an event in Christ and in the Spirit, the spiritual riches of which are inexhaustible.

THE UNINTERRUPTED TRADITION
OF THE CHURCH

Hans Urs von Balthasar

I. The Declaration Touched on All the Decisive
Dimensions of the Problem

The declaration of the Sacred Congregation for the Doctrine of the
Faith on the question of the admission of women to the ministerial
priesthood has prudently touched on all the decisive dimensions of the
problem. It was not afraid to penetrate into the depths of the mystery,
from which such liberating and convincing light shines forth for the
true believer. Certainly, the actual proof which justifies the Church's
way of acting is given in sections 2-4 on the normative way of action of
Christ, then of the apostles and then of the tradition of the Church.
The constancy of this tradition is presented finally not as a "kind of
archaism, but as faithfulness" to her own founder. It is precisely here
that it derives its "normative character."

Only after this primary historical proof does the declaration go on
in section 5 to a thorough consideration of "appropriateness" (*convenientia*), according to the "analogy of faith," as St. Paul called it. But
we must not let ourselves be led astray here by words: where it is a
question of mysteries of the faith, *convenientia* means something quite
different from a mere approximative rightness, or a merely human "suit-
ableness" that might be simply fortuitous and relative. It means rather
what *convenientia* originally meant: coming together, inner harmony,
such as an organism achieves in the balance of its various organs.

The declaration insists expressly on the impossibility of transform-
ing the mysteries of faith into truths considered on the purely rational
plane. Among these mysteries belong also the sacraments, and there-

fore the institution of the ordained ministry in the Church. These mysteries have their own hermeneutics and interpretation, which are accessible and comprehensible only for those who, believing, let themselves be led by the mystery of Christ and the multiple aspects which belong to it in an organic way, into the depths of their inner harmony and plausibility. St. Anselm did not hesitate to attribute a "necessity" to this internal harmony in God, in spite of all the freedom of divine disposition. For even if we must always concede to the sovereignty of God the possibility of acting differently from the way he deigned to act, we have not in any way the freedom to relativize his logic: He is absolute reason, the *logos* itself. Neither have we the freedom to picture in our imagination other ways which he could have taken.

II. Regarding Tradition . . . , Everything Depends on Whether the Aspect in Question Belongs to the Essence of the Structures of the Church

It was necessary to make this premise before being able to tackle in a meaningful way the problem that concerns us. For it is clear *a priori* that the mere fact of a hitherto uninterrupted custom of the Church cannot represent a sufficient proof that this custom could not be changed because of important insights of changed cultural circumstances. If any conclusion is to be drawn from uninterrupted tradition, everything depends on whether the aspect in question belongs to the essence of the structure of the Church, as it was instituted by Christ, or not. There are also other aspects, for which important motives or appropriateness can be indicated, but which can be described only as highly suitable—and not "necessities" in St. Anselm's sense. As an example one could mention priestly celibacy. Although it is possible to point to a long and persistent tradition in such cases, they are not such a central part of the substance of the mystery of the Church. This can be seen from the Pastoral Epistles, in which mention is made of married pastors of local churches. There is also mention of "Peter's mother-in-law." In the Gospel, in fact, Jesus and Paul, in their recommendation of celibacy, merely advise it.

Therefore, argumentation on the basis of the uninterrupted tradition of the Church must necessarily be able to find support in a moment that is contained in the very essence of the structure of the Church and of its sacramentality; a moment preserved from any intervention by the Church to bring about changes (since the latter cannot change at will, but must accept herself, as she was born), and which, in its complete and substantial logic, becomes understandable for faith only if it is considered in the "analogy of faith," in the context of the mystery of the faith as a whole. Now, the essential harmony between the order of creation and the order of redemption belongs to this connection. The redemptive mystery "Christ-Church" is the superabundant fulfillment of the mystery of creation between man and woman, as Paul affirms very forcefully, so that the fundamental mystery of creation is called "great" precisely in view of its fulfillment in the mystery of redemption. The natural sexual difference is charged, *as* difference, with a supernatural emphasis, of which it is not itself aware, so that outside of Christian revelation it is possible to arrive at various deformations of this difference such as, for example, a one-sided matriarchate or patriarchate, an underestimation of women, or, finally, such a leveling of the sexes as to destroy all the values of sexuality. It is only from the indestructible difference between Christ and the Church (prepared, but not yet incarnate in the difference between Yahweh and Israel) that there is reflected the decisive light about the real reciprocity between man and woman.

III. The Concept of Apostolic Succession Is Decisive in the Catholic and in the Oriental Churches

The conferring of the priestly ministry only on men, unchanged in a history of two thousand years, shows clearly enough, as the "declaration" sets forth, that the Church considers it as part of the substance given to her from her very foundation. Particularly important, here, is the testimony of the Oriental Church, which never deviated from the original tradition, although "her ecclesiastical organization admits a great difference in many other problems." And the deviations in the Churches born from the Reformation are quite clearly connected with a changed, weakened relationship between the people of the Church and the apostolic office. This relationship was largely conceived as detached from the concrete succession from the apostles—and therefore also from the structure of the apostolic Church—and constructed directly on the common priesthood of all the faithful.

In the Catholic Church, on the contrary, as in the Orthodox one, the concept of apostolic succession is decisive. The primitive Church was clearly a structured community, because of the ministry set up by Christ for the believing community—with full powers over the authentic proclamation of the word and the administration of the sacraments. And this was to remain so throughout the centuries by means of full powers always transmitted concretely and personally. Continuity with the origin consists, from the Catholic and Orthodox point of view, not only in the faith, but also in the organ responsible for Orthodox faith (and the presence of Christ in the sacraments belongs to this faith): the episcopal office. Even before the existence of a concrete community, Christ at least prepared this office through the calling of the Twelve and the attribution of full powers to them (Mk 3:14f). These "full powers" were already christological: the authorization to proclaim Christ's doctrine in his name and to reject the spirit of the anti-Christ with his power, in the Holy Spirit. This means that here, apparently close to the beginning of his public activity, Jesus granted a participation in his precise messianic function. And this function of the Messiah was, already in accordance with the expectation of the Old Testament, that of representing God and his definitive work of salvation to his people. Hence the apostolic office will always be primarily an office (and, consequently, a responsibility) of representing God, from now on concretely in Jesus Christ.

But representation is a strangely ambiguous phenomenon. It says at the same time something positive: the representative had received from the one he represents full powers to make something of his superiority or dignity present, without being able to claim for himself—and here we have the negative element—this superiority or dignity. This duality makes the concept of representation, and therefore also of the apostolic office, so vulnerable and also so liable to misuse.

In the natural order of the sexes, the representation of God and of his "glory" (*doxa*) is to be found, according to Paul, in the creation of man (1 Cor 11:7). But it is brought home to him how much man is *only* reflection and not the glory itself: "for as woman was made from man, so man is now born of woman. And all things are from God" (v. 12). In the Christian supernatural order, which has its foundation in the natural order, the duality is even more marked; the apostle, as "God's fellow worker," just because he represents Christ, is put "last of all." He is the servant of everyone, who considers it normal that "we are weak, but you are strong. You are held in honour, but we in disrepute" (1 Cor 4:9f).

Now, throughout Catholic tradition and its concept of concrete succession, there passes, at least by underground channels, the awareness of this insuppressible dualism of priestly representation. Even if often, owing to sinful forgetfulness, one-sided emphasis was laid, in a presumptuous clericalism, on the positive aspect of representation—to the extent of the excessive exaltation of the priest as an "alter Christi," which does not exist—yet it has always been recalled too, especially by the saints but also by the ecclesiastical authority, that the apostolic office is only a service for the Church and in the Church, and the service is all the *purer*, the more specific it is. Namely service of the *transmission* of God's gifts, which the priest in no way possesses by himself or even only essentially *in* himself, and which he transmits through his office all the better, to the extent to which he becomes completely a pure instrument of transmission.

IV. Woman Does Not Represent, but Is, While Man has to Represent and Therefore Is More and Less Than What He Is . . .

All this, however, becomes really clear only when one looks at the subject to which the male apostolic service has to dedicate itself: the Church of the faithful of Christ, which—not to mention the Old Testament image of Israel as the bride of Yahweh—is always presented as feminine in the New Testament. According to the major ecclesial reflection, which is well founded on New Testament declarations, this femininity of the Church belongs just as deeply to tradition as the attribution of the apostolic office to man. For patristic theology, as well for the scholastics of the Middle Ages and also of the baroque period, the Church is the mother of the faithful and at the same time the bride of Christ. She stands as the sublime woman in Church portals, as opposed to the crumbling synagogue. In innumerable miniatures, she is presented as the only woman standing under the cross, she holds up the sacred chalice to collect Christ's blood; she is, particularly in Oriental theology, the definitive incarnation of divine Wisdom, who receives and bears in her womb all the seeds of the Logos, dispersed in creation and throughout the history of salvation.

I cannot help thinking here of two books by Louis Bouyer: the first one, *Le Trône de la Sagesse*, is older (1957); the second one, *Mystère et ministère de la femme* (Aubier, 1976) is new and concerns our subject expressly. Its main purpose is to shed light, even more than on the "femininity" of the Church, on the sexual-personal role of woman. While man, as a sexual being, only represents what he is not and transmits what he does not actually possess, and so is, as described, at the same time more and less than himself, woman rests on herself, she is fully what she is, that is, the whole reality of a created being that faces God as a partner, receives his seed and spirit, preserves them, brings them to maturity, and educates them. One can question this thesis of Bouyer in many ways, and we will do so elsewhere. But in the first place its central point is certainly to be accepted, all the more so in that it represents the core of an ecclesiastical tradition, which is free here of all peripheric scoriae and obscurities due to hellenistic misogyny (which is partly re-echoed in the fathers of the Church and in the Middle Ages).

Unfortunately, this liberation and renewal of a great tradition, parallel to that of the sacred ministry, falls in an age in which the whole fruitfulness of the differentiation of the sexes in their respective roles is more and more forgotten and intentionally suffocated. And this in favor of a "masculinization" of a whole civilization, marked by a male technical rationality, a masculinization which is sought under the pretext of equality of rights and parity of the sexes. Inasmuch as the sexual sphere is opened to all technical manipulations, the personal height and depth of the difference of the sexes loses its significance. All "services" are put on the same plane and are therefore interchangeable. Even if man cannot conceive and give birth, why cannot woman carry out in the Church each of these apparently neuter "services" which are entrusted to man?

It is above all this overestimation of the masculine, which object-ivizes the spirit and imprisons sexuality in a low physiological sphere, which today opposes understanding of the attitude of the Church, when she remains faithful to her tradition. Here, too, the principle holds good that "*gratia supponit naturam*." Restored nature would bring to light—within the parity of nature and parity of value of the sexes—above all the fundamental difference, according to which woman does not repre-sent, but is, while man has to represent and, therefore, is more and less than what he is. Insofar as he is more, he is woman's "head" and on the Christian plane intermediary of divine goods; but insofar as he is less, he depends upon woman as a haven of refuge and exemplary fulfill-ment.

It is not possible here, for lack of space, to show in detail this dif-ference in equality of nature; in particular the question would have to be discussed of the masculinity of Christ, in his eucharist, in which he, on a plane above the sexes, gives himself to the Church entirely as the dedicated seed of God—and the participation, difficult to formulate, of the apostolic office in this male fertility, which is above sex. Only if this aspect were fully brought to light, would man's latent inferiority to woman be overcome in some way. But it must suffice to have men-tioned this concept.

V. The Virgin Mary Is the Privileged Place Where God Can and Wishes to be Received in the World

It should give woman a feeling of exaltation to know that she—particularly in the virgin-mother Mary—is the privileged place where God can and wishes to be received in the world. Between the first incar-nation of the Word of God in Mary and its ever new arrival in the receiving Church, there exists an inner continuity. This and only this is the decisive Christian event, and insofar as men are in the Church, they must participate—whether they have an office or not—in this comprehensive femininity of the Marian Church. In Mary, the Church, the perfect Church, is already a reality, long before there is an apostolic office. The latter remains secondary and instrumental in its representation and, just because of the deficiency of those who hold office (Peter!), is so made that the grace transmitted remains unharmed by this deficiency. He who has an office must endeavor, as far as he can, to remove this deficiency, but not by approaching Christ as head of the Church, but by learning to express and live better the fiat that Mary addressed to God one and triune.

As can be seen from all this, the tradition of the Church is far more deeply rooted than might be thought at first sight. It goes down into unfathomable depths, but what we can grasp of it and express in shimmering words shows us that it is within its rights and cannot be challenged by changes in times and opinions (also as regards the role of the sexes).

THE VALUE OF A THEOLOGICAL FORMULA
"IN PERSONA CHRISTI"

A. G. MARTIMORT

There is a tendency today, in certain circles, to stress the fact that the priest, in the liturgy, speaks in the name of the assembly and even in the name of the whole Church. This is a very true and traditional affirmation, which could already be found in the teaching of St. Thomas Aquinas. "In the prayers of the Mass—he said—the priest speaks *in persona Ecclesiae*, occupying the place of the Church."[1] But this statement requires to be explained. It is not, in fact, because the priest would supposedly have been chosen by his community to be its spokesman that he speaks in its name. Furthermore, the prayer he utters goes far beyond the narrow circle of the assembly over which he presides. St. Thomas stated precisely: "Only he who consecrates the eucharist, the sacrament of the universal Church, can represent the whole Church."[2] Pius XII, in the encyclical *Mediator Dei*, thought it necessary to recall: "The priest takes the people's place only because he plays the part of Our Lord Jesus Christ, since Jesus is the head of all his members and offers himself for them. . . ."[3]

That is why one must not be surprised to find often, in the texts of the Second Vatican Council, the formula *in persona Christi* used to characterize the specific way of acting of the ministerial priesthood. Thus we read in the liturgical constitution *Sacrosanctum Concilium*:

---

[1] *Summ. theol.*, IIIa pars, quaest. 82, art. 7, ad 3um; "The priest, during Mass, precisely in the prayers, speaks *in persona Ecclesiae*, on the unity of which he takes his stand."

[2] *In IV Sent.*, Dist. 24, quaest. 2, art. 2.

[3] Pius XII, encyclical *Mediator Dei*, AAS 39, 1947, p. 553 (Denz-Schön. 3850): "We thought it necessary to recall that the priest takes the people's place only because he plays the part (*impersona*) of Our Lord Jesus Christ. . . ."

"the prayers addressed to God by the priest who presides over the assembly *in persona Christi*."[4] In *Lumen Gentium*, the council, wishing to distinguish from the common priesthood of the baptized the ministerial priesthood of bishops and priests, gives the following definition of the latter: "The ministerial priest, by the sacred power he enjoys, moulds and rules the priestly people: Acting *in persona Christi*, he brings about the eucharistic sacrifice, and offers it to God in the name of all the people."[5]

Configured to Christ the Priest

The same Constitution on the Church, a few pages further on, returns to this formula in connection with priests of the second degree, adding, moreover, a new perspective, to which we will come back further on. "By the power of the sacrament of orders, and in the image of Christ the eternal High Priest, they (priests) are consecrated to preach the Gospel, shepherd the faithful, and celebrate the divine worship as true priests of the New Testament. Partakers of the function of Christ the sole mediator on their level of ministry, they announce the divine word to all. They exercise this sacred function of Christ most of all in the eucharistic liturgy or synaxis. There, acting *in persona Christi*, and proclaiming the mystery, they join the offering of the faithful to the sacrifice of their head. Until the coming of the Lord, they represent and apply in the sacrifice of the Mass the one sacrifice of the New Testament, namely the sacrifice of Christ offering himself once and for all to his Father as a spotless victim."[6]

Finally, in the decree *Presbyterorum Ordinis* a more developed expression is found: ". . . that special sacrament through which priests, by the anointing of the Holy Spirit, are marked with a special character and are so configured to Christ the Priest that they can act *in persona Christi capitis*."[7] We find the same idea, if not the same words, several

---

[4]   II Vatican Council, constitution *Sacrosanctum Concilium*, no. 33.
[5]   II Vatican Council, dogmatic constitution *Lumen Gentium*, no. 10.
[6]   Ibid., no. 28.
[7]   II Vatican Council, decree *Presbyterorum Ordinis*, no. 2.

times in this decree: "To the degree of their authority . . . priests exercise the office (*munus*) of Christ the Head and the Shepherd";[8] "By the sacrament of orders priests are configured to Christ the Priest so that as ministers of the Head and co-workers of the episcopal order they can build up and establish his whole body which is the Church."[9]

We have deliberately left in Latin the expression *in persona Christi*. Certain translators of the conciliar texts, however, did not understand that it was a question of a *technical formula*, consecrated by theological tradition, and they misunderstood its exact meaning.[10] Now, the very frequency with which the council utilized it shows the importance it attributed to it for understanding the specific nature of the ministerial priesthood. It will be useful, therefore, to recall its origin and study its significance more deeply.[11]

It was above all St. Thomas who made this formula a classical one. It is often found in his writings. Several times, he refers it to a text of the Second Letter to the Corinthians, which he quotes according to the text of the Vulgate: "*Nam et ego, quod donavi, si quid donavi, propter vos, in persona Christi*" (2 Cor 2:10).[12] It is an evident mistranslation. The Greek is *en prosôpô Christou*, which means "in the presence of Christ" or "before Christ's eyes." However, in spite of the preference he shows for this quotation, the Angelic Doctor can add another one, taken from the same letter: "*Pro Christo legatione fungimur, tamquam*

---

[8] Ibid., no. 6. This formula is already in the dogmatic constitution *Lumen Gentium*, no. 28.

[9] II Vatican Council, decree *Presbyterorum Ordinis*, no. 12.

[10] For example, in the French edition of the council texts published in Paris, Centurion, 1967, p. 397, et passim, it was translated as follows: "*au nom du Christ tête en personne.*"

[11] It is regrettable that B. D. Marliangeas has not published the work he wrote on this subject, of which he gave a brief extract in the collective work *La liturgie apres Vatican II*, Paris, Ed. du Cerf, 1967 (*Unam Sanctam*, 66), pp. 283-288: "*In persona Christi, in persona Ecclesiae, note sur les origines et le développement de l'usage de ces expressions dans la théologie latine.*"

[12] We have found this explanation based on 2 Cor 2:10 four times in the *Summa theologica*: IIa IIae, quaest. 88, art. 12 corp.; IIIa pars, quaest. 8, art. 6 corp.; quaest. 22, art. 4 corp.; quaest. 64, art. 2, obj. 3. It is also found in *Expositio super 2 Cor* cap. 2, lectio 2, ed. Parma 13, p. 309.

Deo exhortante per nos (2 Cor 5:20).[13] This time, it is no longer a mistranslation, nor even an adaptation: the apostle, in fact, exhorting the Corinthians to "be reconciled to God," states forcefully: "Christ gave us the ministry of reconciliation . . . ; that is, God was in Christ reconciling the world to himself . . . entrusting to us the message of reconciliation" (vv. 18-19). It is in the strongest sense, therefore, that its conclusion must be understood: "So we are ambassadors for Christ, God making his appeal through us" (*hyper Christou oun presbeuomen*). The voice of the apostle expresses God's own voice, or rather God speaks the word of reconciliation through the apostle's mouth.

Thus clarified by this Pauline perspective, the formula *in persona Christi* means in the first place that the bishops, successors of the apostles, and the priests, their collaborators, are ambassadors of Christ, that they speak in his name. In this sense St. Thomas also says *ex persona*, an expression he found in the Vulgate in connection with Jephthah's messengers to the king of Ammon (Judges 11:12).

Now, the role of Christ's ministers is not limited to speech, which, in any case, is efficacious in itself, they act in the Lord's name, they carry out his role, they take his place and that not only when they exercise the sacramental ministry proper, but also in the whole of their ecclesial activity. "*Praelatus,*" St. Thomas states, "*in Ecclesia gerit vicem Dei . . . , in persona Dei determinat quid sit acceptum*";[14] "*Christus est caput Ecclesiae propria virtute et auctoritate: alli vero dicuntur capita inquantum vicem gerunt Christi.*"[15]

So "to act *in persona Christi*" is equivalent, therefore, to "take the place of Christ," a formula which we also find again in the decree *Presbyterorum Ordinis* of Vatican II.[16] It is hardly necessary to stress how traditional it is: we find it already in St. Cyprian, in connection with the eucharistic celebration which must obey Christ's institution strictly: "*nam si Christus Jesus Dominus et Deus noster ipse est summus sacerdos Dei Patris et sacrificium Patri seipsum obtulit et hoc fieri in sui*

---

[13] *Summ. theol.,* IIIa pars, quaest. 8, art. 6 corp.
[14] *Summ. theol.,* IIa IIae, quaest. 88, art. 12 corp.
[15] *Summ. theol.,* IIIa pars, quaest. 8, art. 6 corp.
[16] II Vatican Council, decree *Presbyterorum Ordinis*, nos. 12, 13.

commemorationem praecepit, utique ille sacerdos vice Christi fungitur, qui id quod Christus fecit imitatur, et sacrificium verum et plenum tunc offert in Ecclesia Deo Patri, si sic incipiat offerre secundum quod ipsum Christum videat obtulisse."[17] ("For if Jesus Christ, our Lord and God, is himself the high priest of God the Father, and offered himself as a sacrifice to the Father, and ordered this to be done in memory of himself, evidently that priest takes the place of Christ who imitates what Christ did, and he then offers in the Church a true and perfect sacrifice to God the Father if he begins to offer it in the same way in which he sees that Christ offered it.")

Need of Deep Analysis

Earlier St. Ignatius of Antioch, wishing to recommend the sacred ministers to the veneration of the faithful, presented them as taking the Lord's place; it must be confessed, however, that his "typology" is very vague and will transmit its uncertain character to the Oriental treatises on ecclesiastical discipline which succeed one another until the end of the fourth century: "Be concerned to do everything in divine concord, under the presidency of the Bishop, who occupies God's place (*prokathemenou tou episcopou eis topon Theou*), of the priests, who occupy the place on the senate of the Apostles. . . ."[18]

St. John Chrysostom, on the other hand, will give his teaching a more solid foundation by basing it on the Second Letter to the Corinthians.[19] Finally, a commentary on the Byzantine Liturgy, composed in the middle of the ninth century, the *Protheoria*, forestalls surprisingly the terminology of St. Thomas Aquinas. Its formula deserves to be quoted: "If anyone asks how it is possible for the high priests and priests

---

[17] St. Cyprian, *Epist.* 63, 14: ed. Hartel (CSEL 3), p. 713.

[18] St. Ignatius of Antioch, *Ad Magn.* 6, 1 (SC 10, p. 98); again in *Ad. Trall.* 2, 1-3, 1: "You are subject to the Bishop as to Jesus Christ . . . , to the priests as to the Apostles of Jesus Christ. . . . Let everyone revere Deacons as Jesus Christ, as the Bishop, too, who is the image of the Father, and Priests as the senate of God and as the assembly of the Apostles . . . (SC 10, pp. 112-113)."

[19] St. John Chrysostom, *Homil: in 2 Cor,* 5, 20: *PG* 61, col. 477-478.

of today to be mediators of such holy realities, let him know that it is not impossible, especially for those who have this dignity, since *they play the part of Christ* the high priest (*ôs tou megalou archiereûs tou Christou ferousi prosôpon*)."[20]

"To play the part of Christ," that even seems a toned down translation: is there not a discreet allusion here to the mask of the theater, by means of which the actor disappears, giving way to the character whose part he takes? And in this case, is not the same image suggested by the original meaning of the Latin word *persona*? It is necessary, therefore, to make an even deeper analysis of our formula *in persona Christi*.

Explaining the Phrase

In the conciliar texts that we quoted, as also in the *Summa Theologica*, it is above all the priest's role in the eucharistic celebration which is described as being *in persona Christi*. Without excluding the other activities of the priestly ministry, this one is considered the strongest test of the priest's link with Christ.

In fact, both Greek and Latin commentators have stressed the extraordinary nature of the sacrament of the eucharist. Whereas the minister of the other sacraments expresses himself by way of intercession: "Send, Oh Lord, your Spirit . . ." or in an indicative way: "The child so-and-so is baptized . . . ," "So and so, I baptize you . . . ," when it is a question of consecrating the eucharist, the priest proceeds in a historico-narrative manner, a narrative which is action, since the priest completes it with Christ's actions: the breaking and the distribution of communion.[21] Now, in the context of this narrative, the celebrant uses

---

[20] With regard to this text and its twofold version: R. Bornert, *Les commentaires byzantins de la divine liturgie du VIIème au XVme siècle*, Paris, 1966 (Archives de l'Orient chrétien, 9), p. 187. Several times, commenting on the priestly prayers of the anaphora, the author repeats that the prayer *is said in the person of the Lord*.

[21] Readers will note, in connection with the distribution of communion, the reasoning of St. Thomas, *Summ. theol.*, IIIa pars, quaest. 82, art. 3 corp: "It is the priest who distributes the body of Christ . . . , because, as has been said, he consecrates *in persona*

the same words as Christ, quoting them in the first person: "This is my body . . . ," St. Ambrose stressed this in his catechesis for the newly baptized: "All that is said before, is said by the priest . . . ; but when the moment approaches to produce the venerable Sacrament, the priest no longer uses his own words, but he uses the words of Christ; it is the words of Christ, therefore, that produce this sacrament."[22]

Whatever theological discussions were raised later by the Orientals with regard to the *epiclesis*, the western tradition never hesitated: the priest utters Christ's words with the same efficacy as Christ. His personality is therefore effaced before the personality of Christ, whom he represents and whose voice he is: representation and voice which bring about what they signify. *In persona Christi* takes on here an extremely realistic sense which Christian thought has explained in various ways.

In the first place, it has drawn the conclusion that the priest is an image of Christ. It is here that we find again a text of *Lumen Gentium*, already quoted at the beginning;[23] and it is a traditional affirmation, for which it will be sufficient to indicate some witnesses. For example, Narsai of Nisibis who, about the middle of the fifth century, in his XVII homily on the explanation of the Mass, describing the rite of Introit, exclaimed: "The priest who has been chosen to celebrate this Sacrifice, bears in himself at this moment the image of Our Lord."[24] At the beginning of the ninth century, St. Theodore the Studite, disputing with the Iconoclasts, explained the fact that the priest did not use an icon of Christ for baptismal "signatio" as follows: "The priest, standing between God and men, is a replica (*mimèma*) of Christ in the priestly invocations . . . ; being, therefore, an icon of Christ, the priest

---

Christi. Now Christ himself, as he consecrated his body, at the Last Supper, so he gave it to eat to the others also. Therefore, as the consecration of Christ's body belongs to the priest, so its distribution belongs to him."

[22] St. Ambrose, *De Sacramentis*, IV, 14: *SC* 25 bis., pp. 108-111.

[23] II Vatican Council, dogmatic constitution *Lumen Gentium*, no. 28: "in virtue of the Sacrament of Holy Orders . . . they are consecrated in the image of Christ."

[24] *The liturgical homilies of Narsai*, ed. R. H. Connolly, Cambridge, 1909 (Texts and Studies, VIII, 1), p. 4 (ed. A. Mingana, t. 1, p. 273).

plainly does not imitate him by using another icon. . . ."[25] It will be noticed that it is in connection with baptism that Theodore speaks of the priest as the image or replica of Christ: as regards the eucharist, in fact, this similarity marks him for the whole of his liturgical service.

But it is precisely in the eucharist that it must be discovered and understood. In this sense, St. Thomas has a particularly inspiring formula. Having to answer the question: "Is Christ sacrificed in this sacrament?," he comes up against the objection: "In Christ's sacrifice, the same person is priest and victim; but in the celebration of this sacrament, it is not the same person who is priest and victim." He solves it by recalling in the first place that "the celebration of this sacrament is an image which represents the Passion of Christ *(imago repraesentativa Passionis Christi)* and then that, for this very reason, the priest is also the image of Christ: *etiam sacerdos gerit imaginem Christi, in cuius persona et virtute verba pronuntiat ad consecrandum.*[26]

Image—But Also Presence

Not just the image of Christ, but his presence. The Second Vatican Council took up again, in the constitution *Sacrosanctum Concilium*, a statement of the encyclical *Mediator Dei*: "He (Christ) is present in the sacrifice of the Mass, not only in the person of his minister, 'the same one now offering, through the ministry of priests, who formerly offered himself on the cross,' but especially under the eucharistic species."[27]

This is an invitation to understand the nature of the sacrament of holy orders according to the general laws of Christian sacramentalism.

---

[25] St. Theodore the Studite, *Adversus Iconomachos*, cap. 4: *PG* 99, 593.—cf. id., *Epist.* Lib. 1, 11: "The Bishop is a copy *(mimêma)* of Christ, upon whom those following in his footsteps model their lives according to the Gospel. . ." (*PG* 99, 945 D).

[26] *Summ. theol.*, IIIa pars, quaest. 83, art. 1, ad 3um. Cf. *In IV Sent.*, Dist. 8, art. 3, ad 9um: "Because the priest is nearer to the principal agent than the words, since he plays the part . . . ," quoted at greater length below.

[27] II Vatican Council, constitution *Sacrosanctum Concilium*, no. 7 (the quotation is from the Council of Trent, Sess. 22, decr. *De SS. Sacrificio missae*, C. 2):—Pius XII, encyclical *Mediator Dei*, AAS 39, 1947, p. 528.

St. Thomas emphasized forcefully, in the first place, that in the eucharist it is necessary to consider not only the subject matter and the words, but also the priest: "The instrumental power to carry out the change (of the bread and wine into the body and blood of Christ) does not lie only in the words, nor only in the priest, but in both. . . . And as the priest, more than the words, resembles the principal agent (Christ) since he bears his image (*quia gerit eius figuram*), so, to speak simply, his instrumental power is greater and more worthy: moreover, it is permanent and applies to many other similar effects. . . ."[28]

This characteristic which the ministerial priesthood has of representing Christ extends from the eucharist far beyond: "every minister of the Church is, in some way, the figure of Christ (*gerit typum Christi*), as Peter Lombard says,[29] and yet he is superior who represents Christ according to a greater perfection. The priest represents Christ in this, that by himself he carried out a certain ministry; but the bishop in this, that he instituted other ministers, and founded the Church. . . ."[30] In the logic of this reasoning, St. Thomas should have reached the point of admitting the sacramentality of the episcopate and perhaps he would have done so if he had completed the *Summa*.

However, that may be, and to restrict ourselves to the priesthood, the thought of the Angelic Doctor can easily be discerned: the Christian priesthood is of a sacramental nature, not only in the transitory act of ordination, but in the person of the priest. Certainly, the supernatural efficacy of his action as consecrator of the eucharist, or as minister of penance,[31] proceeds from the character received in ordination. But this character is invisible; the priest himself is and must be a sign, and therefore he must confirm the conditions required for that: "*cum sacramentum sit signum, in his quae in sacramento aguntur requiritur non*

---

[28] *In IV Sent.*, Dist. 8, art. 3, ad 9um.

[29] Peter Lombard, *IV Sent.*, Dist. 24, cap. I.

[30] St. Thomas Aquinas, *In IV Sent.*, Dist. 24, quaest. 3, art. 2, quaestiuncula 1.

[31] In the teaching of St. Thomas, it is always *in persona Christi* that the priest pronounces sacramental absolution, although it is formulated in an indicative way: *De forma absolutionis*, c. 1, in *Opuscula omnia . . .* , ed. P. Mandonnet, t. 3, Paris, Lethielleux, 1927, p. 154.—*Expositio super 2 Cor*, cap. 22, lectio 2, ed. Parma, t. 13, p. 309.

solum res sed signum rei."[32] The principal condition is that the sign should have a natural resemblance with what is signified: *"Signa sacramentalia ex naturali similitudine repraesentant."*[33] These two principles are invoked by St. Thomas, as is known, to explain that women cannot receive holy orders.

Degrees of Christ's Presence

From reflection on the testimonies of tradition regarding the ministerial priesthood, it is possible, it seems to us, to draw a certain number of guidelines which can help priests to become more clearly aware of what they are and to discern the respective place of each of their activities.

On the one hand, as we have seen above, it is in all these different activities that they act *in persona Christi* and that they must express his image; but it is from their role in the eucharist that this mystery of identification with Christ is discovered, because it is verified in the most significant way here. Likewise, among the various ways of Christ's presence in the Church, there are, as it were, different degrees, which are enumerated in the encyclical *Mediator Dei*, the constitution *Sacrosanctum Concilium*, and, in an even wider perspective, the encyclical *Mysterium Fidei*.

It is necessary, therefore, to appeal, in the two cases, to analogy, and to start from the first analogue which is the eucharist. In particular, the bond that unites the minister of the sacraments with Christ is different according to the nature of each of them. The sacrament of baptism, in case of necessity, can be conferred even by a pagan, that is, by someone who has not received any character that configures him to Christ's priesthood. Marriage, to be sacramental, requires that bride and bridegroom should have the baptismal character (to say that they are "ministers" is not, it must be added, a completely satisfactory expression). Penance and the eucharist require the character of holy orders.

[32] St. Thomas, *In IV Sent.*, Dist. 25, quaest. 2, art. 2, quaestiuncula 1, corp.
[33] Ibid., ad 4um.

Non-sacramental activities have often been considered so independent of holy orders that the distinction has been made between holy orders and jurisdiction and it has been possible to entrust to laymen certain tasks which in themselves seemed to belong to holy orders. There can be no question here of going into these problems, on which, in any case, the Second Vatican Council has provided elements of clarification. But it was necessary to stress how much the different tasks of the Church imply, each in its own way, participation in Christ's mission and a bond with him which reaches its apex in the eucharistic consecration.

On the other hand and in the same way, it is necessary both to maintain the necessity of these different tasks and to stress that they find their point of arrival and their source in the eucharist. "The other sacraments, as well as every ministry of the Church and every work of the apostolate," the decree *Presbyterorum Ordinis* says,[34] "are linked with the holy eucharist and are directed toward it. For the most blessed eucharist contains the Church's entire spiritual wealth, that is, Christ himself, our passover and living bread. Through his very flesh, made vital and vitalizing by the Holy Spirit, he offers life to men. They are thereby invited and led to offer themselves, their labors, and all created things together with him. Hence the eucharist shows itself to be the source and the apex of the whole work of preaching the Gospel. Those under instruction are introduced by stages to a sharing in the eucharist. The faithful, already marked with the sacred seal of baptism and confirmation, are through the reception of the eucharist fully joined to the Body of Christ."

It is clear that the priest cannot be defined solely by liturgical powers, the principal one of which is the eucharistic consecration. But neither can he be understood without them. He is the one who can lead evangelization to its point of arrival: baptism and the eucharist. He is the one who is associated with his bishop or sent by him to give the seal of unity to the local community through the eucharistic assembly. If he were not involved in the apostolic and pastoral responsibility of his

---

[34] II Vatican Council, decree *Presbyterorum Ordinis*, no. 5.

bishop, he would run the risk of returning to a Judaizing conception of the priesthood. Vice versa, if he did not exercise his sacramental power, he would lose even consciousness of his priesthood and could no longer present to man the true mystery of Christ, accomplished once and for all, but renewed efficaciously throughout the life of the Church. In his person, the priest lives the magnificent paradox of the economy of salvation.[35]

[35] Cf. the conclusion, pp. 219-220, of our study *La testimonianza della liturgia*, in the vol. *Il prete per gli uomini di oggi*. Collective work edited by Gino Concetti, Roma, ed. A. V. E., 1975, pp. 192-220.

THE MYSTERY OF THE COVENANT AND ITS CONNECTIONS WITH THE NATURE OF THE MINISTERIAL PRIESTHOOD

GUSTAVE MARTELET, SJ

At first sight it seems hopeless to look for a connection and even more for connections between the mystery of the covenant and the nature of the ministerial priesthood. It is known, in fact, to what extent the history of the ministerial priesthood in the old covenant was complex, contested, and even contestable owing to cases of unfaithfulness. In spite of admirable examples, such as those of Jeremiah and Ezekiel, who were both priests and who struggled throughout their whole life for the purity and holiness of their function, in spite of the influence of those who drew up the code of holiness and the various priestly documents in the Pentateuch, in spite, above all, of the unequaled prestige of Aaron, the brother of Moses, it is clear that the priestly function in the Old Testament had to suffer a great deal from the attraction exercised on men by honors, power, and profits of every kind. Even in the definitive structure of the priestly order, which will be in force from Josiah to the ruin of the temple, Israel will keep the memory of the idolatry that the priests of the high places, ancestors of the "Levites" of the temple, encouraged cynically, it seems, if we are to believe Hosea and even more Amos. As a result the Levites were integrated in a lower rank in the priestly caste, and Ezekiel invites them to remember their past iniquities, to explain this discrimination of which they are still the object.

Then, too, the priests of the line of Zadoc, of better spiritual origin, will not be much more edifying. Ezekiel once more is scandalized by the way they secretly worship reptiles and the sun, even inside the temple (8:12). It is to them that the Lord of hosts is not afraid to say in Malachi: "I will curse your blessings," even adding: "I will spread dung upon your faces, the dung of your offerings" (2:2-3). Nor can it be forgotten that, in the time that precedes the coming of Jesus, the priestly caste had compromised itself with the political power to such an extent that the Qumran sect had seceded, in view of a spiritual reform, imbued with Messianism. In short, the testimony of the old covenant bears no less on the defects of the priests than on the importance of their functions, particularly with regard to the sacrifices (Lev 16) and, for a certain time, to the Law (Deut).

In light of the New Testament, and, in particular, the Letter to the Hebrews, it is the very function of the Aaronic priesthood which is criticized, as compared with the unequaled greatness of the priesthood of Jesus. The now ascertained weakness is no longer only a *contingent* matter, related to "good" and "bad" Levites, it is clearly *structural:* it depends on the very nature of the Old Testament priesthood. The author of the Letter to the Hebrews says bluntly: "If perfection had been attained through the Levitical priesthood . . . what further need would there have been for another priest to arise after the order of Melchizedek, rather than one named after the order of Aaron?" (7:11). The fact is that the mystery of Christ has now fully revealed that the whole priestly edifice of the Old Testament was—as St. Paul says in another context—"only a shadow of what is to come" but that "the substance belongs to Christ" (Col 2:17).

What is it about, in fact, this mystery of the covenant which the Old Testament inaugurates without being able to complete it, if not the possibility, to use St. Paul's words again, of "access in one Spirit to the Father" (Eph 2:18)? A possibility which only the person of the Son can offer not only to Jews but also to pagans, since *all* nations were blessed in Abraham, with whom the covenant began. Certainly, it was necessary for everything to begin with the flesh, in order that man might really be touched by God. It is not angels in fact but men who are of flesh and blood like Abraham (Heb 2:16) that Christ assists and must deliver by "bringing many sons to glory" (Heb 2:10, 16). Under these conditions, however, questions were raised which were evidently insoluble for men, however qualified they might be. It was a question of fulfilling a promise that was apparently impossible to keep: that God might be able to delight in a people who would see in "knowledge and love of God"—as Hosea says (6:6)—its faithfulness and "worship." Then not just "the country" would be filled with knowledge of God, as Isaiah promises in the marvelous apocalypse of chapter 11, but from every part of the earth, according to Malachi, "incense and a pure offering" (1:11) would be offered. This offering of oneself in love of God evidently presupposes, in Israel and in the whole of humanity, a kind of fantastic recasting of the heart which would pass, as Ezekiel announced, from the order of stone to that of flesh, and then from the order of flesh to that of the spirit (33:26).

Jeremiah, too, had spoken unforgettable words on his point, which the Letter to the Hebrews could not but quote to drive home the unequaled originality of Christ, who accomplished their content: "This is the covenant, that I will make with the house of Israel after those days, says the Lord: I will put my laws into their minds, and write them on their hearts, and I will be their God, and they shall be my people. And they shall not teach every one his fellow or every one his brother, saying, 'Know the Lord,' for all shall know me, from the least of them to the greatest" (Jer 31:33-34, quoted in Heb 8:10-12). A marvelous new covenant, indeed, which will make knowledge and love of God an instinct which is born with the heart and grows with it!

For such a prophecy to be fulfilled, we said, a recasting of the whole of mankind would be necessary. The prophecies of the Servant of the Lord give us the presentiment that this recasting will take place at the beginning, only in a really extraordinary subject, unique in his kind. We divine from the prophecy that the way in which "this promised man" will recapitulate men in himself and cause "God's arm" to triumph in them, alone capable of molding and remodeling humanity, however rebellious it is, will not be biological in the first place. By means of the biological element, in fact, Adam was able to transmit only a spiritually frail heritage, which vanished, in any case, rapidly. Abraham himself saw his descendants torn apart. As for David, his carnal love for Bathsheba led to the division of his kingdom! It will be necessary, therefore, that the one who has to teach God's justice even to the most distant islands should take man in a specifically spiritual way. Bound to us, thanks to a birth that integrates him fully in the human plane, he will also have to be so imbued by the Spirit as to be able, in the offering of himself and in his simplicity, in the uprightness and marvelous patience of his heart, to gather and recapitulate in himself the whole of mankind, which the division of the pastures and the lying multiplicity of the pastors scatter in the wind.

This awaited man, this "messenger of the covenant in whom you delight," to use the expression of Malachi (3:1), is the entirely new man, the perfect man, the second and last Adam, as St. Paul calls him. He is not a meteorite who has nothing to do with our earth, not an intruder, but a man who rises from the earth, a shoot, the branch, as Zechariah says (3:8). While he bears within him all man's authenticity, since, as the second Adam, he is connected with the first, he also contains in himself (this is the paradox) all the newness of God, all the hidden power of the Spirit, who conceived him, moreover, in the Virgin's womb. In him the new covenant is no longer just a promise, of which he is the prophet, but a reality: "all the promises of God find the Yes in him; in him it is always Yes," as St. Paul says (2 Cor 1:19). Having received, in his flesh, in his blood, in his whole humanity, the Spirit, "without measure" (cf. Jn 3:34), he speaks, lives, loves, offers himself, dies, and rises again, renewing completely the cycle of life and death which he traverses like us, in fact better than us, transfiguring it without disfiguring it. In this way he can breathe on us the Spirit which is his, as the Son of God living forever in our flesh.

I said "breathe," according to the text of John (20:22). Exegetes, in fact, are now paying renewed attention to the apparition Jesus made to the eleven, which this evangelist reports in this passage. We are informed of this detail, enlightening for faith, that is, that the Risen Christ "breathed" on his disciples. The verb used here is almost an exception in the Bible. It is found only in the narration of creation of man. What God did for the first man, breathing upon his face the breath of life, Christ, the second Adam, this "lifegiving spirit" as St. Paul says (1 Cor 15:45), does also for those that he does not disdain to call his brothers and friends. In this way he brings them into the completely new life, which is his, that is, the life of the Son himself, which makes possible complete communion with God and, therefore, with others. The free "access to the Father in the Spirit" is now opened to all men by the Christ of the Resurrection, who is also the Christ of the Pentecost, who, returning to the Father, gives us his Spirit (cf. Acts 2:33). The fruits of this Spirit can and must rise over the whole of mankind, like a new spring the sap of which no winter could deaden.

What God Has Promised Is, Therefore, Fulfilled

In what does this new covenant, which Jesus found in his person, donor of the Spirit to his Body, the Church, and through her, to the whole universe, in what does it still imply a priesthood? Compared with this High Priest, who is reconciliation itself and the unfathomable renewal of man, does not every other form of priesthood melt like snow in the sun? Who can claim in fact to fill an office that is in the slightest an addition or a supplement or a help to the strictly personal mission of Christ? Who can liberate himself from sin but the Liberator himself? Who can open the way towards the Father but the Son in our flesh? Who can make men "worshipers in spirit and in truth," who can spread among his followers the Spirit in whom we can cry: "Abba! Father"? Who, but the One who, incorporating us in his life in the Church, permits us to repeat in the Spirit that animates it, the words of perfect oblation and absolute renunciation: "Sacrifices and offerings thou has not desired. . . . Then I said, 'Lo, I have come to do thy will, O God'" (Heb 10:6).

Now this communication of Christ's oblative sonship to all the members of his body is so deep and complete that the priesthood became in Christ no longer a *particular institution* but *the very form of the life of the whole Church*. This is the meaning of the famous words in the First Letter of Peter, the extreme newness of which nothing must ever compromise: "Come to him, to that living stone, rejected by men but in God's sight chosen and precious; and like living stones be yourselves built into a spiritual house, to be a holy priesthood, to offer spiritual sacrifices acceptable to God through Jesus Christ" (2:4-5). Here the priesthood is not in the first place *a special ministry* or *a function*, it is *a baptismal state of life* or if you like *a charism of existence*, which defines every Christian. This aspect of things is so clearly manifested in the Scriptures that our Protestant brothers are unable to go beyond this evident fact, which, however, implies something which is not affirmed in this place but which nothing excludes or denies.

A ministry of "priestly" institution and function does, in fact, spring from the new covenant, provided we are willing to see in it a depth of which Christ is the marvelous realization.

When the prophets reproach Israel with her infidelity in terms of prostitution—remember the famous twenty-third chapter of Ezekiel—they are speaking literally, for in the covenant God actually became the bridegroom of his chosen people. The text of the Congregation for the Doctrine of the Faith recalled this so clearly that I can be content with an allusion here. The covenant is, therefore, a mystery of such deep union between the Lord God and the members of his people that the conjugal life of man and woman is still only an image of the tradition, extraordinary in itself, which defines the Lord as a fiancé, a bridegroom, and Israel as a fiancée and a real bride, though unworthy.

To express the mystery which he realizes with the filial communication of the Spirit to his body, the Church, Christ does not reject such a symbolism. As is the second Adam, the one who assumes and recapitulates in himself the whole truth of the first Adam, so he is also the perfect bridegroom, which the first one had difficulty in becoming in an order much more modest. The Church is consequently the bride who receives and shares entirely the very life of Christ. So that the new covenant is a perfectly successful marriage, in Christ and the Spirit, between God, who receives from us the humanity which is ours, and ourselves, who receive from him the divinity which is his.

Here is precisely the foundation of a quite specific ministry, which can be called priestly in the real sense of the word. In fact this astonishing communication between Christ, the bridegroom, and his Church-bride defines the Church of Jesus Christ so much that the latter can rightly take up again and apply to herself the Son's words to his Father, to express her unity with Christ: "all mine are thine, and thine are mine"

(Jn 17:10). In fact, there is no separation of the body, far less divorce, there is no room even for reserve in the "tradition" that Christ assures her of himself, in the truth of the Gospel, in the life of the resurrection, in the revelation of secrets of the kingdom. There is nothing that can make the Church think that Christ has withdrawn or is withdrawing himself from her in the order of truth proclaimed evangelically, of transmitted sacramental life, of spiritual existence transformed day by day in her history. Everything is given, everything is transmitted, everything is handed over, nothing is kept. There is no reservation when it is a question of Jesus Christ giving himself to the Church. "You will even do, Jesus says to his followers, greater things than I have done myself," that in particular of going to the frontiers of the world, of which I have known only Galilee or at least Palestine and some bits of Decapolis. This nuptial communication of his life, this surrender of the whole of himself into the hands of his Church, so that we may thus live of the Spirit, is at the same time the value of the Church and her identity.

But the depth of this gift must not mask the identity of the donor. Love for the bride must not annihilate the personality of the bridegroom. The complete community of property between Christ and his Church must not give rise to a gradual cancellation of Christ. Having become invisible with his resurrection, he must not, however, become evanescent in the visibility of a Church which, having to administer the property of her bridegroom, should reach the point of veiling him or—even worse—of supplanting him gradually. This is an inadmissible prospect, which urges us to consider things differently and say everything in a positive way. The Church, in fact, needs to know always that the riches which she so miraculously has for herself and for the life of the world are nothing but the property of her Christ, and Christ himself. Hence the necessity for her to possess, in her living reality as a society unique in the world, the irrefutable *sign* that everything she possesses, everything she enjoys, she receives incessantly from Christ and from him alone. Now, since Christ, having become invisible for her, can no longer appear personally to affirm his irreplaceable presence and action, there will be in the Church a visible and efficacious reminder of her absolute and vital dependency on her irreplaceable bridegroom. The ministerial priesthood is this sign.

An institutional charism given by the bridegroom to the body of his bride, so that the latter may always see in him the author of the love that surrounds her, the ministerial priesthood is, in the Church, a primary visible element of the person of the Lord. Its value is not related to the persons who exercise this function, which is disproportionate from every point of view to their qualities and their defects; it depends entirely on the objective gift of Christ in the Spirit, which thus sets up men in a function in which greatness and simplicity are mingled. They are, actually, one of the efficacious signs of the irrefutable identity of the absent one and therefore of his action. Thus the Church can see and know in faith, thanks to this social, functional, and public sign, that Christ has not vanished within her. In the moment of complete communication between the bridegroom and the bride, which is, as is known, the eucharist, the climax of the espousals of the whole Church with Lord, the Church can understand that everything she lives on, quenches her thirst with, and nourishes herself on, comes from Jesus Christ. He is, so to speak, standing in her midst in the efficacious sign of a ministerial priesthood, the whole value of which is to be the visible actuality of him who freely gives himself to his Church in this way. The ministerial priesthood signifies, therefore, in a public way for faith, that the bridegroom, with whom the bride deeply desires to unite, is a Christ that she can take only because he offers himself. So Christ, who has given himself entirely as life and love of his body, maintains towards the Church the personal distinction of the bridegroom, who is the very source of the goods which he lavishes upon her.

There can be no question of tackling here, far less solving them, all the problems that this ministry implies. I wished merely to show its deep logic, by making its existence spring from what is most remarkable and astonishing in the new covenant. What explains best, in fact, the existence of a ministerial priesthood in Christ's mystery is not the priesthood of the Old Testament, as was sometimes clumsily suggested in the Middle Ages, but the incomparable originality of Jesus

Christ. A simple remark will enable me to emphasize this point, in conclusion.

It will be remembered that one of the great concerns of the christological councils of the East was to avoid the twofold danger, contradictory and symmetrical, of a unity of the two natures in Jesus Christ that would be confusion, and of a distinction that would become opposition or conflict. Now, this concern can be transposed to illustrate the union between Christ and the Church. The mystery of the new covenant establishes—as we have seen—a nuptial relationship of bridegroom-bride between Christ and the Church. It, too, implies a union without confusion and a difference without opposition between Christ and the Church. In fact, if Christ is not the Church and likewise the Church is not Christ, each one having his or her own personality, they are both inseparable, as are the bridegroom and bride in a perfectly united couple. There is, therefore, a distinction of persons between Christ and the Church, without separation, however, since the Church is really the body of Christ and Christ is fully himself only through the Church his bride.

Certainly, only the Spirit can guarantee this perfect union in the purest distinction, which, moreover, excludes all opposition as well as all confusion. The fact remains, however, that the ministerial priesthood exercises, by virtue of the Spirit, a function that can easily be distinguished in the economy of salvation. While Christ, with the gift of himself, guarantees the Church a union that abolishes all spiritual distance, which would leave the Church with her hunger unsatisfied, it is necessary for the bride herself, however, to possess within herself the sign that reminds her efficaciously of the incomparable personality of the bridegroom. Since union always presupposes the real difference of persons, theirs will be all the deeper and more successful: all confusion excluded, no distance, however, will be established, but only the distinction which guarantees union will be signified. In this sense the ministerial priesthood, beyond all merit of the subjects invested with it only to serve the whole Church, helps the Church not only not to forget the conditions of her union, but even more to rejoice always in the originality of a bridegroom whose marvelous singularity is incessantly recalled to her by the consecrated ministry.

Finally, since it is a question of a ministry which depends entirely on the identity of the bridegroom, it can be understood that the priestly service of the new covenant should be carried out by men. Are they not by nature bridegrooms and not brides? Man is, therefore, better suited than woman to symbolize in the conjugality that defines the communion of the new covenant the bridegroom from whom the bride knows she receives both love and life.

THE MINISTERIAL PRIESTHOOD AND
THE ADVANCEMENT OF WOMEN

✠ Joseph L. Bernardin

In execution of a mandate from Pope Paul VI and echoing a declaration which the Holy Father himself made in a letter of November 30, 1975,[1] the Sacred Congregation for the Doctrine of the Faith has issued a Declaration on the Question of the Admission of Women to the Ministerial Priesthood reaffirming that the Church "in fidelity to the example of the Lord, does not consider herself authorized to admit women to priestly ordination."[2]

The Sacred Congregation admitted that this is a position "which will perhaps cause pain," but expressed confidence that its "positive value will become apparent in the long run, since it can be of help in deepening understanding of the respective roles of men and women."[3] The pain will be most intense in those Catholic quarters where studies and discussions have seemed to favor the possibility of women priests. Such is the case especially in the United States of America.

In this article, I wish to discuss the Sacred Congregation's declaration on ministerial priesthood in relation to the more general question of the advancement of women. Although this process is developing at an uneven pace throughout the world—in public, professional, and intellectual life and even within families—it is part of the renewal and humanization of society and of the Church. Thus we must reflect upon the immediate and the longer range results of the reaffirmation by the

---

[1] *AAS* 68 (1976), pp. 599-600; cf. ibid., pp. 600-601.
[2] Sacred Congregation for the Doctrine of the Faith, Declaration on the Question of the Admission of Women to the Ministerial Priesthood (referred to in the following footnotes as declaration), October 15, 1976, Edition of Vatican Polyglot Press, p. 5.
[3] Ibid.

Sacred Congregation of the Church's constant teaching as it affects the advancement of women.

Immediate Problem

First we must face the immediate problems. Bishops, to whom the document is primarily addressed, have the mission of explaining it to their people in a pastoral way according to their knowledge of the people whom they serve. This will require joint efforts by bishops and priests, who share the ministerial priesthood, to enter into the thoughts and feelings of others. It will be important for them to understand and to take into consideration the sensitivities of women, their feelings and inclinations, their manner of approaching religious matters and reacting to them.

Women, for their part, and those who are working for the advancement of justice for women must try to appreciate the import of this declaration in a positive fashion. Those who favor the ordination of women will need to examine the clear teaching of the magisterium on this matter. The question impinges too directly on the nature of the ministerial priesthood for it to be resolved within the framework of legitimate pluralism between churches.[4]

It is important that we enter into dialogue with open minds and open hearts. The theme "ministerial priesthood and the advancement of women" is given different meanings and stirs up different feelings in different people, men and women, clergy, Catholics and Protestants, believers and non-believers. It would be good if everyone could give the same meaning to the same words. The magisterium has clarified what the Church understands by the term ministerial priesthood and why women are not called to this office. Now we must see how this understanding can influence and advance the role of women in the Church and society.

---

[4] Commentary on the Declaration on the Question of the Admission of Women to the Ministerial Priesthood (*L'Osservatore Romano,* English-language edition, 3 February 1977).

Longer range strategies and tactics for the full assimilation of the profound relationships between the Church's teaching on the ministerial priesthood and the advancement of women require patience, but a form of patience different from merely marking time. Rather, the appropriate attitude is one which recognizes that God accomplishes his designs through men and women, and, further, that in all great projects time is necessary for their maturation. St. Paul admonishes us that "sufferings bring patience, as we know, and patience brings perseverance, and perseverance brings hope" (Rom 5:4, 5).

Need for Patience

Patience of this kind is particularly suited to efforts for the advancement of women to their right and proper place within the Church, society, and family. This is especially true if we see the advancement of women as a long process of convergence bound up with an inner renewal of each of these three interrelated communities in accord with the requirements and demands of each.

The most urgent thing at the present time is, as Pope Paul has pointed out, "the immense task of creating awareness and of bringing about the advancement of women at the grassroots level, in civil society and also in the Church."[5] More than ten years after the publication of the *Pastoral Constitution on the Church in the Modern World* it is a sad fact that "fundamental personal rights are not yet universally honored. Such is the case of a woman who is denied the right and freedom to choose a husband, to embrace a state of life, or to acquire an education or cultural benefits equal to those recognized for men."[6]

Those called to the ministerial priesthood have special reason to promote the advancement of women because of the attitude of Jesus,

[5] Holy Father's Address to the Members of the Study Commission on the Role of Women in Society and the Church and the Committee for the Celebration of the International Women's Year, April 18, 1975 (*L'Osservatore Romano*, English-language edition, 1 May 1975).

[6] Pastoral Constitution on the Church in the Modern World (*Gaudium et Spes*), no. 29.

an attitude carefully maintained by the apostolic community. If Jesus did not call women to be part of the Twelve, "it was not in order to conform to the customs of his time, for his attitude toward women was quite different from his milieu and he deliberately and courageously broke with it."[7] In embracing the cause of justice for women, ordained ministers express the unselfish love of the Lord.

Bishops and priests can take encouragement and direction from meditating on the several examples of Christ's attitude cited by the declaration: the great astonishment of his own disciples when he converses publicly with the Samaritan woman (Jn 4:27); Jesus takes no notice of the legal impurity of the woman who had suffered from hemorrhages (Mt 9:20-22); he allows a sinful woman to approach him in the house of Simon the Pharisee (Lk 7:37); by pardoning the woman taken in adultery, he means to show that one must not be more severe toward the fault of a woman than towards that of a man (Jn 8:11). He does not hesitate to depart from the Mosaic Law in order to affirm the equality of the rights and duties of men and women with regard to the marriage bond (Mk 10:2-11).[8]

Women in the Ministry of Jesus

Women should ponder the extraordinary opportunities that Jesus afforded to women to accompany him on his itinerant ministry and to give first testimony to the resurrection: "Mary, surnamed the Magdalene, from whom seven demons had gone out, Joanna the wife of Herod's steward Chuza, Susanna, and several others who provided for them out of their own resources" (Lk 8:2-3). Contrary to the Jewish mentality, which did not accord great value to women's testimony, it was women who were the first to have the privilege of seeing the risen Lord and who were charged by him to take the first paschal message to the apostles themselves (Mt 28:7-10; Lk 20:11-18).[9]

---

[7] Declaration, p. 6.
[8] Declaration, pp. 6-7.
[9] Ibid., p. 7.

This brings us to a fundamental observation which is emphasized in another way by the commentary on the declaration by the Sacred Congregation: we must not expect the New Testament *on its own* to resolve definitively the possibilities for ministry of women in the Church or of the Church and her ministers in promoting the advancement of women.[10] The Scriptures do not enable us to give a full account of certain of the sacraments of the Church, and especially the sacrament of order. "But it must be recognized that we have here a number of convergent indications that make all the more remarkable the fact that Jesus did not entrust the apostolic charge to women."[11]

The New Testament does not give us a blueprint for the advancement of women nor finished structures of ordained ministry. But it does offer profound insights into what may be the most necessary aspect of the work of reconciliation in our day: that an essential condition for being an instrument of God's plan is *unselfish love*. The ideal, in practicing ministry, in advancing a cause, in dialogue, is to achieve the greatest possible selflessness.

These considerations lead us to the consideration that there are different functions within the Church: the quality of Christians harmonizes with the complementary nature of their tasks. Sacramental ministry is not the only rank of greatness, nor is it necessarily the highest. Rather it is a form of service. "The greatest in the kingdom of heaven are not the ministers but the saints."[12]

The deeper understanding of Christian life and ministry which flows from prayerful study of the declaration makes clear the need for spiritual progress and for the assuming of urgent apostolic tasks. "There is a universal vocation of all the baptized to the exercise of the royal priesthood by offering their lives to God and by giving witness for this praise."[13] While the priesthood does not form a part of the rights of the

---

[10] Commentary (*loc. cit.*).
[11] Declaration, p. 7.
[12] Ibid., p. 18.
[13] Ibid., p. 17.

individual, but stems from the economy of the mystery of Christ and his Church,"[14] the priestly office also "cannot become the goal of social advancement; no merely human progress of society or of the individual can of itself give access to it: it is of another order."[15]

Concrete Suggestions

If we seek in the declaration a plan of action, we discover that there are concrete suggestions. "In the final analysis it is the Church, through the voice of her magisterium, that, in these various domains, decides what can change and what must remain immutable. When she judges that she cannot accept certain changes, it is because she knows that she is bound by Christ's manner of acting. Her attitude, despite appearances, is therefore not one of archaism but of fidelity; it can be truly understood only in this light."[16] Our plan of action, therefore, must begin from and in fidelity to this decision. We must move forward from this sure and certain starting point and get on with what is required to promote the advancement of justice for women.

Within the Church, for example, much can and should be done to develop official ministries for women, especially in cases where as a matter of fact they are already doing the work which the particular ministry would entail. One thinks, for example, of the service rendered by women as catechists and ministers of music. Studies of ministerial roles open to women have already been undertaken by some episcopal conferences and by the Holy See. In its commentary the Sacred Congregation noted that there were "deaconesses" in the early days of the Church, although the nature of their status is not clear. The commentary stated that the question of the diaconate "must be taken up fully by direct study of the texts, without any preconceived ideas; hence the Sacred Congregation has judged that it should be kept for the future."[17] This study will shed more light on the role of women in the early Church

---

[14] Ibid.
[15] Ibid.
[16] Ibid., p. 11.
[17] Commentary (*loc. cit.*).

and give insights as to how women might participate in the Church's ministry of service today.

The call to spiritual progress is given to every priest and bishop by the declaration as a condition for the effectiveness of their apostolic tasks. "The priest is a sign, the supernatural effectiveness of which comes from the ordination received, but a sign that must be perceptible and which the faithful must be able to recognize with ease."[18] The whole sacramental economy is based on natural signs; "the same natural resemblance is required for persons as for things."[19] The "natural resemblance" between Christ and his ministerial priests must not stop merely with the fact that they share a common masculinity. The ministerial priest acts not *"in masculinitate Christi"* but *"in persona Christi."* If he is to be an effective sign, especially if he is to lead and inspire others, particularly women, in the apostolate, then he must display the virtues and the godlike qualities of the man Christ. It is not maleness which must be accented and brought forward as the significance of the priesthood, but rather Christlike qualities: humility, gentleness, self-effacing service must be easily recognizable.

Biblical Symbolism

In the beautiful biblical symbolism of the unity of all in Christ the declaration presents a plan of reconciliation to remedy the divisive effects of sin: "there are no more distinctions between Jew and Greek, slave and free, male and female, but all are one in Christ Jesus (cf. Gal 3:28)."[20] The nuptial mystery, which is the great sign of both the Old and the New Covenant, presents God as related to the chosen people, who are seen as his spouse; Christ is the bridegroom, the Church is his bride. "It is through this scriptural language, all interwoven with symbols, and which expresses and affects man and woman in their pro-

---

[18] Declaration, p. 13.
[19] Ibid.
[20] Ibid., p. 13.

found identity, that there is revealed to us the mystery of God and Christ, a mystery which of itself is unfathomable."[21]

For this plan of reconciliation to be effective the sacramental renewal of the events of salvation which were achieved in the incarnation and the paschal mystery of death and resurrection must take place. The ministerial priest must preside and celebrate these mysteries. Here it is not so much the priest as a man who presides, but it is Christ who is priest and victim.

In this plan of divine reconciliation and within the biblical and ecclesial sacramental signs and symbols we can find a new way of looking at the advancement of women and at the progress and development of peoples. This was a central thought of the message of Pope Paul VI to "the Special Study Commission on the Role of Women in Society and in the Church" (May 3, 1973): "Baptism and confirmation of themselves constitute the essential sacramental bases which confer on lay people—men and women—the fullness of their Christian vocation and make them capable of sharing, as lay people, in the Church's apostolate."[22] By the paschal mystery, by baptism, God's people, women and men, have been removed from the situation of sin. One is struck especially by the reversal of perspective and the novelty of the evangelical outlook which integrates women into society with men on a basis of equality.

"Equality, development, and peace," the theme of the 1975 International Women's Year, evokes a lively interest from the Church. Pope Paul addressed the Church's Secretary General for the International Women's Year: "Equality can only be found in its essential foundation, which is the dignity of the human person, man and woman, in their filial relationship with God, of whom they are the visible image."[23] Equality does not exclude distinctiveness and special contributions which

[22] The Special Study Commission on the Role of Women in Society and in the Church (3 May 1973).

[23] The Holy Father's Address to Mrs. Helvi Sipila, assistant secretary general for development and humanitarian affairs and secretary general for International Women's Year (1975), 6 November 1974 (*L'Osservatore Romano*, English-language edition, 14 November 1974).

women can make to the full development of society according to their individual callings and talents. But pursuing this distinctiveness in unity, the pope continued, "the woman of today will be able to become more conscious of her rights and duties, and will be able to contribute not only to the elevation of herself but also to a qualitative progress of human social life, 'in development and peace.'"[24]

Nature of Real Equality

Equality of the baptized is the key to finding the proper apostolic roles for women today. "It therefore remains," the declaration concludes, "for us to meditate more deeply on the nature of the real equality of the baptized which is one of the great affirmations of Christianity: equality is in no way identity, for the Church is a differentiated body, in which each individual has his or her role."[25] We must, however, do more than meditate upon this equality, this unity in diversity, this beautiful plan of reconciliation and peace: we must work to actualize them.

If we perceive the plan of reconciliation inherent in this declaration, we shall discover that women's advancement does not depend merely on prominent ecclesiastics or activists whose names appear in the daily newspapers and on radio and television. The personal efforts of each one count. The Nobel Peace Prize winner Father Dominique Pire, the Belgian Dominican who worked in behalf of refugees after World War II, wrote: "I think that to be a peacemaker, that is a man of peace, one must first be at peace with oneself. In other words, one must first achieve inner peace. This involves getting to know oneself and learning to control one's impulses. Only then can a peaceful being approach the immense task of creating harmony between groups and individuals."[26]

The problems of equality for women involve longstanding hatreds and oppressions. We are dealing with the ravages of sin, sins from the

---

[24] Ibid.
[25] Declaration, p. 17.
[26] D. Pire, *Building Peace* (London: Transworld Publishers, 1967), p. 108.

beginning of human history and sins which are still being committed. Although the task is arduous and the ultimate hopes far in the future—perhaps it will be verified that "one man sows; another reaps" (Jn 4:37)—it is not true that the Catholic Church has ignored this problem or is just beginning to solve it.

Advancement of Women

Pope Paul VI, commenting on the theme of IWY, "equality, development, and peace," pointed to the Catholic Church's involvement in these goals. "Already nearly twenty years ago (not to mention still earlier periods) our predecessor Pius XII said to the women of the whole world: 'You can and must make your own, without restriction, the program of the advancement of women—a program which upholds with an immense hope the unnumbered throng of your sisters who are still subjected to degrading customs or who are the victims of poverty, of the ignorance of their milieu, and of the total lack of means of culture and formation' (Address to the World Union of Catholic Women's Organizations, 29 September 1957)."[27]

If the advancement of women has been conceived so far "in Christian terms" and "in the light of faith" it is certainly not to diminish its scope. In the same message to the IWY conference at Mexico City, the Holy Father wrote: "It will suffice for us to mention just one sphere which we have particularly at heart: the campaign against illiteracy, the illiteracy which plays an evil role, especially among women in rural areas, constituting an obstacle to development and offending essential rights, for, as we recalled in our encyclical *Populorum Progressio*, 'hunger for education is no less debasing than hunger for food: an illiterate is a person with an undernourished mind.'"[28]

In its last paragraph the declaration makes a strong plea for women to carry Christian values with them into all sorts of services for the

[27] Message of His Holiness Pope Paul VI to Mrs. Helvi Sipila, secretary general of the International Women's Year, Mexico City, 19 June-2 July 1975 (*L'Osservatore Romano*, English-language edition, 3 July 1975).

[28] Ibid.

good of humankind: "The Church desires that Christian women should become fully aware of the greatness of their mission: today their role is of capital importance, both for the renewal and humanization of society and for the rediscovery by believers of the true face of the Church."[29] Now that the question of ordination to the priesthood has been resolved for the Roman Catholic Church it will be more free to promote the advancement of women at all levels.

Bishops and priests especially must approach energetically and sensitively the challenge of opening to women positions in the Church which do not require ordination but which have been normally handled by the ordained in the recent past. Over a longer period of time such a course of action will be a strong force in removing some of the pejorative connotations which have been associated with the term "clericalization" of the Church's ministry.

Discrimination Still Exists

In a more general way it must be admitted that some clergymen do not really appreciate the feelings of alienation which many women in all ranks of society experience and feel deeply. We must recognize the truth of Pope Paul's comment in his address to the final session of the Study Commission on the Role of Women, January 31, 1976: "It is true that in many countries, theoretically at least, men and women have already acquired the same fundamental rights. But discrimination still exists."[30] Women must enjoy equality not just in theory but in practice.

In his address to the Study Commission the Holy Father calls for all to respond to their responsibilities: "Authentic Christian advancement of women is not limited to the claiming of rights. The Christian spirit also obliges all of us, both men and women, to remember always

---

[29] Declaration, p. 18.

[30] Address of His Holiness Pope Paul VI to the Study Commission on the Role of Women in the Church and Society, and to the Committee for the International Women's Year, 31 January 1976 (*L'Osservatore Romano*, English-language edition, 12 February 1976).

our own duties and responsibilities. Today it is especially a question of achieving a greater and closer collaboration between men and women, in society and in the Church, in order that all 'will contribute their individual talents and dynamism to the building up of a world that will not be leveled down to uniformity but harmoniously unified' (*AAS* 67 [1975], p. 265). The advancement of women, understood in this way, can be a powerful aid to the achievement of unison between people and to the establishment of peace in the world."[31]

In many places studies are being undertaken to explore and develop possibilities for new ministries for women. Experiments with "team ministries" of men and women, clergy and laity, religious and lay, etc. have been successful in many places. We need to be alert to new fields of activity and responsibility which are everywhere open to Christian women. The results of innovative programs should be shared with the Church at large.

Finally, the biblical analogies of the nuptial imagery which are suggested by the declaration as arguments for the fittingness of limiting the call to ministerial priesthood to men suggest comments on marriage and the dedicated life of single women and vowed religious. "I will espouse you in right and in justice, in love and in mercy: I will espouse you in fidelity, and you shall know the Lord" (Hos 2:21-22). "Husbands love your wives, as Christ loved the Church. . . . This is a great foreshadowing; I mean that it refers to Christ and the Church" (Eph 5:25, 32).

Women's Role in the Home

The permanent sacramental bond of matrimony is still the great sign of God's covenant love, and it is still proper to speak of women's role in the home. Although raising and educating children should be a joint effort of father and mother, the role of the mother is essential. The meaning of the great and beautiful sacramental image of the love of

[31] Ibid.

husband and wife and the analogy of faith with the doctrine of the mystery of the Church would be less than appropriate, if Christian marriages were not indissoluble and irrevocable as God's love is for his people. Furthermore, the examples of unselfish love and dedication which husbands and wives give to one another and to their children inspire generosity and love on the part of ministerial priests for Christ and his Church, for his brothers and in the ministry and for the people he serves.

Single women, especially those with professional training, are the most obvious ready source of talent from which the Church can draw help for her apostolates. Unfortunately, this group is most likely to feel the effects of discrimination and alienation. Often these women have theological training which ought to be fully recognized and used in the service of the Church. The fidelity of those women to Christ and to projects on behalf of humanity merits the promise of Hosea's prophecy: "I will espouse you in fidelity, and you shall know the Lord" (Hos 2:22).

The consecrated religious woman (or man) remains the privileged sign of espousal with the Lord and should be of all the most totally available for the work of the Gospel. In the past religious have been eminently free and willing to go to the ends of the earth to bear the message of salvation. Although the declaration does not specifically mention religious, the theme "ministerial priesthood and the advancement of women" is a challenge to a more selfless life of service. By their life, their prayer, their apostolate, religious are in a special position to mediate the pain and suffering which some may experience in reaction to the declaration of the Sacred Congregation. The ranks of religious orders and congregations are likely to be beneficiaries of the long-term deepening of the appreciation of man and woman which the Sacred Congregation anticipates as the fruit of its work.

This declaration by the Holy See calls all of us to serious reflection upon some central elements of our belief and the obligations which arise from them. Such reflection will enable us to see how much more, beyond a simple prohibition, it is really saying to us. In particular, the obligation to work for the advancement of women in society and the Church becomes more urgent, not less, in light of this clear and authoritative reaffirmation concerning women and the ministerial priesthood.

THE MALE PRIESTHOOD:
A VIOLATION OF WOMEN'S RIGHTS?

✠ Joseph Ratzinger

The restriction of the priestly and episcopal ministry to men was clearly reaffirmed by the declaration *Inter Insigniores,* as the expression of the whole tradition of the Church. Faced with this fact the objection particularly raised today is that this is a violation of the fundamental equality of rights and dignity of men and women. This equality of fundamental rights of all human beings, which was first expressed in the early documents of the North American nation in formation, and was founded on the Christian belief in creation,[1] was expressly confirmed by the Second Vatican Council: "Forms of social or cultural discrimination in basic personal rights on the grounds of sex, race, color, social conditions, language or religion, must be curbed and eradicated as incompatible with God's design."[2] The declaration mentions this text, but does it not, at the same time, tacitly contradict it?

In order to be able to give an answer, we must clarify the conceptions in question. We must explain what a fundamental right is and what the priesthood is. Only then can we establish whether the priesthood can be numbered among the fundamental rights in which a differentiation of the sexes is "incompatible with God's design."

Without having to lose ourselves in the difficult discussion of the problem of fundamental rights, we can note that, from the historical point of view, there are two principal forms in which the concept of fundamental right emerges.

We have already referred to the Anglo-Saxon type with its Christian foundation. Its essential idea can be described as follows: the con-

---

[1] Cf. W. Wertenbruch, *Menschenrechte,* in *RGG* II (3) 869f.
[2] *Gaudium et Spes,* nos. 2, 29.

cept of fundamental right is inseparably bound up with the idea of creation. For creation alone can be the basis of rights which underlie all historical institutions and are binding on them in advance. Fundamental rights are, therefore, in the first place those claims of the human being which are the consequence of his origin in creation. Fundamental rights are rights bestowed by creation and that is the reason for their unconditional equality and their strictly necessary character for everything that has a human face.

With the declaration of the rights of man of the French Revolution, there appears, on the other hand, a new form of "human rights" the full significance of which became evident only in the course of time and which is taking over from the Christian form more and more today. According to this form right appears as a merely human institution. From man's understanding of a suitable organization of human society, he lays down what is to be valid as right. The premise here is that man, behind whom there is no creative will, has reality completely at his disposal and, in proportion as his reason grows, sets himself the task of seeking the most rational and therefore optimal organization of reality. The institution of right is therefore a means of rational mastery of the world. Human rationality is the source of right, which is formed by the will of the majority and is progressively improved. Here rationality is opposed to authority and since in this case everything is continually decided by the majority, it is just and necessary that everyone should take part in the same way in the process of the formation of opinion and the formation of the majority.

Summing up we can say: the concept of fundamental right is derived either from belief in creation or from the conception of the "constructability" of the world and its functionality in the context of human reasoning. It is not necessary to say here that the council accepted only the first form of the concept of fundamental right and confirmed it as the doctrine of the Church; nor do the different consequences of the two principles concern us here.

What happens if we apply this model to the question of the priesthood? Well, first and foremost it should be clear that the Christian priesthood is not something that is immediately derived from the order of creation or that is the right of the human being as a human being. If we wish to speak in a broad sense of a priesthood emerging from creation, then it certainly belongs to man and to woman, each in his and her own way: in the unity of the couple they are called to be bridges to the Creator for each other. As human beings they are called to carry on the testimony of creation and to join in that message which invests the whole of creation: "The heavens are telling the glory of God . . ." (Ps 19[18]:2). Expressed in other words: the vocation of the human being—man and woman—is to complete the silent worship of creation and thus bring back creation to its origin. But all this does not concern us here, although it is certainly not out of place to mention this original vocation of man, which the Christian faith has not eliminated, but deepened and made concrete.

Let us establish, therefore, that the Christian priesthood is not a consequence of creation. Neither has it anything to do with any kind of equality of supernatural destiny. As is known, St. Augustine was even of the opinion that the priesthood, with its immense responsibility, made salvation more difficult to attain rather than easier.[3] Therefore this first examination of the context must give rise to the suspicion that the bringing up of human rights in matters of the priesthood betrays a dulling of the sense of the "supernatural," of the new, non-deducible, and specific aspect of Christianity.

But, it will be objected, in this way the sense of the argumentation is completely misunderstood. We do not think at all of claiming the priesthood as part of the order of creation: the principle of equality refers not simply to realities that belong to every human being. The principle under discussion refers then to the exclusion of disadvantages on account of sex, no more no less. In fact the conferring of the priesthood on both men and women is defended in Protestant circles, which are certainly far from the concept of deriving the priestly ministry from creation. In their argumentation it is understood that the priesthood

---

[3] See in *Lumen Gentium*, no. 32 the well-known passage (St. Augustine, Serm. 340, 1: *PL* 38, 1483): "When I am frightened by what I am to you, then I am consoled by what I am with you. To you I am the bishop, with you I am a Christian. The first is an office, the second is a grace; the first a danger, the second salvation."

appears as an institution of the Church, which she must regulate according to the points of view of opportuneness and observing the principle of equal opportunities. In this way the Church herself is seen as a functioning apparatus and her relationship to right is conceived in the perspective of the concept of right of Enlightenment. If this were so, if the priesthood were a possibility to be conferred and freely regulated by the Church, then there would really be a corresponding right to this possibility and the prohibition of the priestly office for women would be a clear case of prejudice "on account of sex," something which Vatican II expressly opposed.

But is it really so? With this question we have arrived at the second problem mentioned above: what is the priesthood in its essence? This question could be answered at once very simply: according to the tradition of the Catholic faith (which on this point may perhaps partly contradict Protestant conceptions) the priesthood is a sacrament. This means: it is not a mere profession at the disposal of the Church as an "institution" but is an independent, preexisting datum. The sacrament has, with regard to the Church, a position similar to natural law with regard to the civil legislator. It reveals immediately what is specific and different in the ecclesial institution as compared with secular institutions of every kind and level. On the one hand the sacrament constructs the Church as an "institution," a constituted reality *sui generis,* only because of the sacrament. On the other hand the sacrament does not belong to the sector of her institution that the Church can change at will. Rather it sets a limit on her free disposal of herself, a limit in which her fundamental task must be faithfulness to her mandate.

The conflict about the question of a new formulation of the conditions of access to the priestly ministry is seen here, in the last analysis, as a dispute between the functionalist conception of law and the sacramental conception of the Church. In this connection we can first ask the question whether the complete victory of functionalism, which assigns all rights to the institution and regards planning rationality as the only determinant yardstick, can in the long run lead to a victory of woman and her rights; we will come back to this later. For the moment we must keep in mind that the Church cannot just act regarding herself as she likes and that the priesthood is not an opportunity that she can assign on her own authority. It is not to be considered in the sense of an opportunity or a right, but is to be seen as a vocation which no one can claim as a right and which cannot be simply bestowed by the Church either (even though a vocation is not complete without the consent of the Church). In the course of the vocation the call through the Church is certainly part of the process, but this call of the Church can construct only on the call of God and it finds as one of the measures of this the aforesaid fundamental structures of sacramental tradition.

It could be objected now: very well, the Church does not invent the sacraments but finds them already there. Nevertheless, a considerable area of action is left to the Church and it is just this area of action that should be exploited here, for nothing proves that being male belongs to the inalienable substance of the priesthood. There is every likelihood, on the contrary, that it is a question of a concession to times bygone which are now obsolete. Now, it is correct that no one can bring forward compelling metaphysical proofs to show that the priesthood can only be as it is and not otherwise. Anyone who says so is taking too much upon himself. The declaration *Inter Insigniores* rightly points this out too (no. 5): it does not wish to give a proof from which it follows that things must be so, but tries to understand the admittedly contingent fact from the inner structure of faith. But this contingency belongs to the way of constructing of Christian faith in general, which is based on the history of salvation and therefore on accidental elements which would be quite conceivable in other forms. No one can prove that the Word of God could become man only precisely in Palestine and precisely in the times of the emperor Augustus. On principle, of course, it would be conceivable and "possible" in another way. No one can prove that Christianity then had to spread first to Europe, and so on. The Protestant theologian J. J. Von Allmen has developed this thought very well in connection with the species of the eucharist: why should the Church celebrate the Lord's Supper everywhere and in all times with the typical food of the Mediterranean? The answer lies in the fact that "the initiative of the Supper does not come from the Church," "because it is Christ himself who lays the table, and when he invites us to table, then it is he, too, who should choose the food. . . . The eternal Son of God came as Jesus of Nazareth, to bring salvation to all men. When he 'converted' men to this being-a-Jew . . . , he called upon them to accept the fact that he cannot be recognized unless in this period far away in the past. . . . Because in a certain sense one cannot but become a Jew when one becomes a Christian, these elements . . . , i.e., the bread and wine, must be respected. . . ."[4]

The direct connection with this history, the connection with God's concrete will for salvation, as it took form in this history, belongs fundamentally to the essence of the sacrament. In faithfulness to what is "accidental," the connection is established with what is indispensable in God's action for us. In this, too, lies clearly the limit of the action of the Church in the sphere of the sacraments, of which the declaration *Inter Insigniores* speaks very effectively in no. 4. The Church acts, but she acts upon preexisting elements. In the last resort only she herself can distinguish between substance and what is changeable, but it is precisely in this distinction that she experiences that she is bound. Moreover the declaration in question has shown in a convincing way that the argument that Israel, Christ, and the apostles had yielded here to contemporary necessities just does not hold water (nos. 2 and 3). L. Bouyer has set out this problematic even more thoroughly and with regard to the affirmation of a choice motivated by historical reasons, he said in his drastic way: "One feels one is dreaming when one hears men, who consider themselves enlightened and free of all prejudice, come out with such impossible things."[5] "An argumentation of this kind is sheer nonsense."[6]

Let us establish, therefore, that the priesthood is no opportunity on the professional plane and so there is no corresponding right. It is

---

[4] J. J. van Allmen, *Okumene im Herrenmahl* (Kassel, 1968), 48f. Actually, van Allmen wastes the fruit of his consideration in the end when he tries again to justify in one way or another the thesis that the Church is free to do as she likes.

[5] L. Bouyer, *Mystère et ministère de la femme* (Paris 1976), 12.

[6] Ibid., p. 21. See also p. 23: Mais, dans le cas présent, aussi bien, le massif *consensus fidelium* (de plus de vingt siècles) est appuyé sur une surabondance, en réalité, d'enseignement biblique et d'expérience spirituelle chrétienne qui ne peut échapper qu'à una vue myope des textes et des faits.

from the theological standpoint not a bestowing of a privilege on anyone, but a sacrament, the expression of the historical faithfulness of the Church to her origin, which precisely in its "accidental" historical form is the concrete expression of God's action for men.

At the same time, however, something else must be said. If these affirmations, incontestable on the theological plane, are to convince people in actual fact, the priesthood in its empirical form must correspond to the theological idea and must continually be purified of any appearance of being a privilege. Indeed, any appearance of privilege has been renounced when, historically, the priesthood was lived purely: in missionaries, in all the messengers of divine love, ever wearing themselves out and consuming themselves for the word.

We might perhaps content ourselves with what has been said, but the concept of the sacrament is not yet exhausted. The sacrament is, in its essence, symbolical representation, the making present in symbols of a concealed reality. Only in this way does its contrast with a rationalistic, functionalistic outlook emerge clearly. For rationalism, everything that exists is fundamentally "material," which man causes to "function" and sets him up as a function in his activity. The equality of the whole of reality is based on its total functionality, that is, on the fact that "function" becomes the only category of thought and action. The sacrament, on the other hand, knows preexisting symbolic structures of creation, which contain an immutable testimony. The symbolic place of man and of woman also falls within this interpretation of reality; they both have equal rights and equal dignity, but each has a different testimony. It is just this that functionalism cannot admit, for its complete activism implies also complete equality, in which everything receives its definition only from the activity of man himself.

L. Bouyer has rightly pointed out that this type of equality through uniformity actually contains the sole dominion of the male form and produces equality through the negation of woman.[7] It is significant that the two qualifications in which the particular way and dignity of femininity is expressed in an unchangeable way—virginity and mother-

[7] Ibid., 23-27.

hood—should be slandered and ridiculized in an unprecedented way today. In other words: the two fundamental ways of being in which woman, in a way granted to her alone, expresses the high point of being human, have become forbidden concepts and anyone who brings them positively into action is suspected *a priori* of obscurantism. In other words, in this form of the concept of equality what is specifically feminine is, in the last analysis, forbidden. One can find in it a masculinization of unprecedented proportions, within which a Manichean feature can easily be discerned: the human being is ashamed of the sexual, of his masculinity or femininity, because here is something which eludes complete planning and modeling and binds him to his created origin. The sexual is therefore deliberately relegated to the purely biological and the latter is then treated as not belonging specifically to humanity (which means "rationality"). Licentiousness is fundamentally a Manichean contempt for man's biological roots, which must be pulled out of the human. This Manichean spiritual slant is paid for by woman in the first place: the incarnation of the spirit, which constitutes what is specific in the human being, the peculiar characteristic of this creature of God called man—this incarnation of the spirit is manifested in her in a more radical and essential way than in man. It is easier for him to limit fatherhood to a biological parenthesis than is possible in the case of motherhood; it is easier for him to escape from the preconstituted structure of created life to the fictitious emancipation of operating rationality than it is for woman. The Manichean slant contained in all this is tantamount to the destruction of the human, the denial of the creature, man, and above all the denial of the femininity of woman. Behind the mask of emancipation, of the attainment, at last, of equal rights, is concealed complete assimilation and contestation of the right of being a woman and just in this way being supremely a human being.[8] Of course to say so does not mean to deny that prejudice really exists and that the struggle for equality of opportunity is justified. The danger lies in the fact

---

[8] Cf. Bouyer, *op. cit.* See also the important article of the Viennese pediatrician H. Asperger, *Kind und Familie. Moderne Modelle,* in: *Communio* 2 (1973) (German edition).

that what is justified may so easily serve as a vehicle for what is destructive and untrue.

But what has all this to do with our subject? It would be too simple to want to tack these dangers onto the question of the priesthood for woman. This is not the question. What is important, on the other hand, is the confrontation between functionality and symbolic representation as the limit of functionality. And from what has just been said the following should be clear: the defense of the symbolic representation, on which the decision of the Congregation for the Doctrine of the Faith is based, is the defense of woman offered for today. Indeed the defense of the person as a person before the overall claims of technology and its contempt of creation. Though it may not seem so at first sight, it is a question here of woman's right to be herself, not in an equivocal equality which considers the sacrament as a career and so changes it into a dish of lentils which is not worth buying.

In conclusion, we must add once more that the finest ideas remain incredible, and are even falsified, if the facts of the Church's life do not correspond to them—if the priesthood really becomes a career and if woman's service does not find in the Church its proper scope, its own greatness and dignity. Herein lies the important task which the declaration *Inter Insigniores* sets the Church today.

CHURCH'S PRACTICE IN CONTINUITY
WITH NEW TESTAMENT TEACHING

Albert Vanhoye, SJ

I

In the declaration *Inter Insigniores* of October 1976, the Congregation for the Doctrine of the Faith presented in a simple, precise, and nuanced way the New Testament data that could shed light on the question of the non-admission of women to the ministerial priesthood. This manner of presentation guarantees that sixteen years later the text retains its validity. On the other hand, it is also possible to complete it on some points, taking into account the most recent discussions. This article intends to do precisely that.

The text of the declaration does not appear one-sided; on the contrary, it covers the various aspects of the situation. On the one hand, it noted some essential facts: although Jesus appeared completely free of bias or prejudice regarding women, he "did not call any woman to become part of the Twelve" (*Inter Insigniores*, no. 2); after the resurrection, "the apostolic community remained faithful to the attitude of Jesus" (ibid., no. 3); later, although the spread of the Christian mission to the hellenistic world could have produced "within the apostolic Church a considerable evolution vis-à-vis the customs of Judaism, . . . at no time was there a question of conferring ordination on women" (ibid.). These facts have fundamental significance, in the sense that they are at the origin of the Church's constant tradition in East and West, which did not allow that women could validly receive priestly or episcopal ordination.

The declaration, however, unhesitatingly acknowledges that these facts, although fundamental, are not alone sufficient to resolve the question. The reason is that the New Testament does not consider the problem explicitly and hence does not provide us with any "immediate evidence" in the matter. No New Testament text, that is, expresses a prohibition of women being ordained. On the other hand, the later organization of ministries in the Church was the result of a long evolution that brought many changes unforeseeable at the time the New Testament was written. So it remains possible, humanly speaking, to imagine some further changes in the sacrament of orders too.

A careful ecclesial discernment is necessary, however. The reason is that, for such a change to be allowed, it is not enough for it to conform to the evolution of cultures and mentalities (let us remember that St. Paul urged Christians, "Do not conform yourself to this age" [Rom 12:2]), it is not enough for it to correspond to a certain idea of women's rights in a democratic society; it is first of all necessary for the Church to acknowledge the suggested change as an element of the homogeneous growth of Christ's body and not an injury inflicted on this body, or an abnormal, unhealthy development. Therefore, the declaration rightly concludes the discussion by saying: "In the final analysis it is the Church, through the voice of her magisterium, that, in these various domains, decides what can change and what must remain immutable" *(Inter Insigniores*, no. 4). In regard to the possible ordination of women, the discernment that the Church very carefully made had a negative outcome: "The Church, in fidelity to the example of the Lord, does not consider herself authorized to admit women to priestly ordination" (ibid., Introduction).

II

The declaration does not say much about "the example of the Lord." It merely observes that "Jesus did not entrust the apostolic charge to women." It would have been possible to give greater attention to Jesus' decision by recalling that, according to Luke, this decision was prepared for by a whole night in prayer (Lk 6:12) and so was done "through the Holy Spirit" (Acts 1:2), a fact that clearly excludes the possibility of the decision being determined by the customs and prejudices of the time. Mark states precisely that Jesus "summoned those whom he wanted" (Mk 3:13). In the discourse after the Last Supper, one of Jesus' statements emphasizes that aspect of the event: "It was not you who chose me, but I who chose you" (Jn 15:16). These gospel data are in some way reflected in the passage from the Letter to the Hebrews that says in regard to the priesthood: "No one takes this honor upon himself but only when called by God" (Heb 5:4). All these observations represent a pressing appeal for the Church's magisterium to take cognizance of the extreme importance of this issue and to respect with complete fidelity the direction taken by Jesus, refusing to claim the power to change this direction, regardless of the pressure brought to bear or the arguments advanced.

Nevertheless, it must be acknowledged that the position occupied by the Twelve in the Church has a unique form and, consequently, what is valid for the Twelve is not necessarily valid for other church ministries. In this regard the New Testament leaves many things unclear. For example, it does not specify how the "presbyters" we see associated with the Twelve in leading the Jerusalem Church were chosen and instituted (cf. Acts 15:2, 4, 6, 22). On the point at issue we nevertheless note a few facts:

1. When Judas had to be replaced after the ascension, Luke states that Peter expressly limited the choice to "men" (andres in Greek: Acts 1:21) who had accompanied Jesus during his public life, although some women at the time had stronger claims since they had been more faithful to Jesus than his male disciples, even on Calvary and at the tomb (Mt 27:55, 61; par.). The first to receive the proclamation of the resurrection, they also received the mission of passing the news on to the apostles themselves (Mt 28:6-7; par.). In spite of this, the possibility of choosing one of them was not considered. The names of two men who were never mentioned in the Gospel accounts were proposed (Acts 1:23).

2. Later, when the increased number of disciples caused problems in the community and required a more diversified organization of the ministry, the Twelve likewise invited "the community of the disciples" to select for the new task "seven men (andres)" (Acts 6:3), even though

the problems concerned female groups, those of the widows (Acts 6:1). In this account the laying on of hands is mentioned (Acts 6:6) as the ordination gesture for a ministry. It meant—and still means—the bestowal of a spiritual power conferred by God.

3. In the New Testament women never receive this laying on of hands. The cases mentioned concern only men: Barnabas and Saul in Acts 13:3, when at the Holy Spirit's command they were sent on an apostolic mission, and Timothy, in 1 Tm 4:14 and 2 Tm 1:6, texts which speak of a "gift of grace *(charisma)*" conferred by this rite. Similarly, the texts that give directions for choosing presbyters (Ti 1:5-6) and the *episkopos* (1 Tm 3:2) state clearly that it is a question of men *(andres)*.

III

Anyone wanting to advocate a change contrary to the Church's constant tradition, despite these clear observations, cannot cite any explicit New Testament text, but only some details of uncertain and disputed interpretation (for example, the titles *diakonos* and *prostatis* given by St. Paul to a Christian woman in Rom 16:1-2). Others try to show that Jesus founded a community of "equals," in which absolutely no attention was paid to the difference between women and men. The assertion is then made that the Church soon began to depart from this ideal and the New Testament, although preserving some traces of the original orientation, now reflects the return to a "patriarchal" system that oppresses women.

As a vestige of the original orientation the sentence in Gal 3:28 is usually cited in which St. Paul says: "There is neither Jew nor Greek, there is neither slave nor free person, there is not male and female; for you are all one in Christ Jesus." Far from ignoring this text, *Inter Insigniores* repeatedly underscores it, quite rightly noting, however, that "this passage does not concern ministries: it only affirms the universal calling to divine filiation, which is the same for all." Since feminist reasoning has paid little attention to this detail, it is appropriate here to reaffirm its correctness.

This is clearly seen when the text of Gal 3:28 just quoted is compared to that of 1 Cor 12:13, which says: "For in one Spirit we were all baptized into one body, whether Jews or Greeks, slaves or free persons." Some exegetes do not see any great difference between the passages; a feminist exegete even uses 1 Cor 12:13 to confirm the traditional, pre-Pauline nature of Gal 3:28. In reality, the perspectives of the two passages are radically different; while the phrasing of Gal 3:28 is repeatedly negative, that of 1 Cor 12:13 does not contain any negation. While Gal 3:28 denies the differences, 1 Cor 12:13 lets them stand. In fact, both the preceding and subsequent context asserts that they are necessary. The preceding verse actually points out that the body "has many parts" (12:12); the following verse says: "Now the body is not a single part, but many" (12:14). The apostle then strongly insists on the necessary diversification of the parts to ensure the different vital functions of the body.

Anyone wanting to interpret the meaning of these two texts correctly must pay the greatest attention to their different perspectives. The Letter to the Galatians discusses the *foundation* of Christian *existence.* On this basic level only one thing counts: faithful adherence to Christ. The "works of the law" do not matter, nor do individual differences, whether religious, social, or sexual in origin. United to Christ through faith, all are "one." On the other hand, the First Letter to the Corinthians considers another level, that of the various *functions* carried out in the Church, the body of Christ. At this secondary level, St. Paul affirms the necessity of the differences. Not everyone can be an apostle, not everyone prophets or teachers (cf. 1 Cor 12:29-30). These differences, established by God himself (12:28), are to be accepted by each person for the good of the whole body. They are the conditions for a life of effective charity. Egalitarian claims, however, cannot be reconciled with authentic charity because they are in accord neither with the divine disposition contained in creation (cf. 1 Cor 12:18) nor with the example of Christ in redemption (cf. Phil 2:6). Of course, all Christian men and women are equal in their fundamental dignity. "For through faith you are all children of God in Christ Jesus" (Gal 3:26). However, it does not follow that all have a claim to the same functions within the Church.

As for the attempt made several years ago to base an egalitarianism upon a "feminist theological reconstruction of Christian origins," it is unfortunately necessary to say that it is without theological validity because, instead of accepting the testimony of the New Testament, it adopts a "hermeneutics of suspicion" in regard to it. That is, in studying the writings of the New Testament, it takes as a point of departure the "suspicion" that their authors more or less consciously hid their egalitarian leaning, which was supposedly the tendency of Jesus and his first disciples. Consequently, they claim to reconstruct this "authentic" orientation through the unilateral use of some clues found in the texts, completing them with many conjectures, often directly contrary to other New Testament texts. Such a method is obviously not capable of providing the Church with a sure foundation for changing one of her traditions in such an important area. A reconstruction based on historical conjecture is completely out of place in this matter. The only valid foundation is perfect obedience to the word of God.

IV

In summary, regarding the question of not admitting women to priestly ordination, I believe it is necessary to state that no new element of importance has been brought forward by New Testament exegesis in recent years. We must say again that the New Testament does not explicitly treat this problem. It would be anachronistic to expect it to furnish a solution. However, an unbiased study of the texts leads one to recognize that, on the one hand, the assigning of ministries is a very important fact in God's eyes, and that the Church's ancient tradition of not admitting women to ordination is in continuity with the data of the New Testament. On the other hand, the New Testament shows that the basic equality of all the baptized in no way requires that the functions entrusted to women in the Church should be identical to those entrusted to men. All are children of God (Gal 3:26) and all are called to "serve one another through love" (Gal 5:13). It is not important that the way of "serving one another" is not the same for everyone.

The only thing that matters is that man and woman should fulfill the service that is theirs "in love."

CHURCH'S STANCE CONTINUES THE PRACTICE OF CHRIST AND THE APOSTLES

✠ Inos Biffi

1.   Although several years have gone by since the Congregation for the Doctrine of the Faith published its declaration *Inter Insigniores* on the admission of women to the ministerial priesthood (October 1976), it still retains its value regarding both the formulation of the terms of the question in their concrete context and the dogmatic references involved in its "authoritative and official," although not infallible solution: in addition to this, later interventions by the magisterium, for example, *Mulieris Dignitatem,* confirmed it.

Two contexts are recognized as the motivation behind the question of admitting women to the ministerial priesthood: the more general one of the demand for women's advancement with their assumption of increasingly visible and significant roles in public life; the other, more specific one of the emphasis on the presence of women in the Church's life and activity.

Having accepted the necessity and value of this advancement as such, *Inter Insigniores* shows the new "theological" relevance of a conclusion which would signify and consequently entail the admission of women to priestly ordination. In fact, the only valid perspective for correctly determining the problem is the "theological" one which, on the one hand, has no prejudice for or against the issue and, on the other, does not allow itself to be based on cultural or anthropological reasons that are extraneous to the criteria by which a topic involving the Christian mystery and praxis should be judged and solved.

2.   The critically assumed theological reason or the dogmatic place of considered discernment is the one fundamental for Christian hermeneutics: tradition, where in various forms, including calm conviction, the Church's authentic consciousness is at work and is revealed.

In our case, with a unanimity that resisted other divergences and with a stability that was in no need of explicit intervention, the Church "has never felt that priestly or episcopal ordination can be validly conferred on women" (*Inter Insigniores*, no. 1), with the conviction that in this she remains "faithful to the type of ordained ministry willed by the Lord Jesus Christ and carefully maintained by the apostles" (no. 1).

Now in this same stability and unanimity the Church does not reveal a decision of her own, but her obedience to and dependence on Christ and the apostles, who did not give her the competence to "manage" the sacraments beyond the substance assigned to them by the one who instituted them.

Apostles Remained Faithful to Jesus' Attitude

3.   As for Jesus Christ, it can be clearly seen that his new and original behavior in regard to women was profoundly liberated from Jewish cultural conditioning: "His attitude towards women was quite different from that of his milieu, and he deliberately and courageously broke with it" (no. 2). Despite this, *Inter Insigniores* observes, he "did not call any women to become part of the Twelve" (no. 2), and even his mother was not invested with the apostolic ministry.

Nor is any difference to be seen in the practice of the apostles, who "remained faithful to the attitude of Jesus" (no. 3). They also distanced themselves from anti-feminist attitudes, displaying a noteworthy evolution in this regard. Nevertheless, we never find them asking if ordination should be conferred on women; in spite of the important role played by women and their substantial cooperation, in apostolic times they did not perform a public, official function which always belonged "exclusively to the apostolic mission" (no. 3).

4.   Indeed, it is a question of seeing what significance should be attributed to the behavior of Jesus and the apostles.

Some people have held, and still do, that it is merely the result and an indication of non-binding cultural and "historical circumstances," in much the same way as some New Testament prescriptions about women are not considered normative. Even further, according to some a change in this regard would be legitimate, and would be in the Church's power to foster, as she has done with other aspects of the sacraments down through the centuries.

Similar objections, the most frequently recurring ones, refer us back to the essential questions: what binding force should be attributed to the attitude of Jesus and the apostles? Would it be within the Church's authority to change the subject upon whom sacred orders is conferred?

5.　The response cannot come from any voice other than that of the Church's magisterium, whose task it is to discern what is unchangeable in regard to the sacraments or what represents their substance, and what can change; in other words between what corresponds to Christ's intention and what belongs to a variable discipline, obviously distinguishing between essential "fidelity" and archaism.

According to *Inter Insigniores*, the Church's tradition in this regard, with its characteristics of stability and unanimity, shows an objective magisterium, according to which the conferral of priestly ordination on men alone is normative in nature rather than disciplinary. In this case the practice or the fact has the weight of dogma: Jesus and the apostles expressed a norm that they "considered to conform to God's plan for his Church" (no. 4). Introducing a different usage would amount to the Church's superiority to and independence from Jesus Christ, whose *"potestas"* is at all times decisive and determining for the Church herself, which is called to be faithful to him.

6.　Since a sacrament is involved, this is the basis, and the only possible basis, of the reason why women cannot be ordained. Our document clearly and pointedly recalls "that problems of sacrament theology . . . cannot be solved except in the light of revelation" (no. 6). The human sciences or historical plausibility cannot be decisive: "One cannot see," the document states, "how it is possible to propose the admission of women to the priesthood in virtue of the equality of rights of the human person, an equality which holds good also for Christians" (no. 6).

This would mean failing to recognize that the Church herself cannot be compared to other groups, because she is "a society different from other societies, original in her nature and in her structures" (no. 6).

Nor can people appeal to the fact that in Christ there is no distinction between men and women: this means that all are called in the same way to divine filiation, and "does not concern ministries" (no. 6).

Symbolism of Priesthood Refers Immediately to Christ

By improperly including sociological or anthropological reasons, one would fail to recognize that priestly ordination cannot be equated with a right that men and women alike could claim. In such a perspective priestly ministry would be totally misunderstood: It is "not conferred for the honor or advantage of the recipient, but for the service of God and the Church. . . . (It) does not form part of the rights of the individual, but stems from the economy of the mystery of Christ and the Church. The priestly office cannot become the goal of social advancement; no merely human progress of society or of the individual can of itself give access to it: it is of another order" (no. 6); more precisely, it is of a "theological order" or profile, which is all too often missing from reflections on the topic and which has not lost any of its validity.

7. The intervention by which the Congregation for the Doctrine of the Faith presented the doctrinal references for the question of the ministerial priesthood of women also offers us a reflection on the "profound fittingness" between the mystery of Christ and the fact that only men are called to receive the sacrament of orders: it is an example of *intellectus fidei,* which does not create but rather seek to "justify" and illustrate the theological principles and the solution derived from them. As is known, it is intrinsic to "sacred doctrine" to try to find the *rationes* for the content of the faith. According to *Inter Insigniores*, against the background of the relationship between Christ, the head and bridegroom of the Church, his body and bride, one can "understand" how it is a man who, through ordination, is constituted to represent Christ, that it is a man and not a woman who is to act in his name—*in persona Christi;* to be his image; and even more so, one can see the "plausibility" that the incarnation of the Word took place according to the male sex, with a choice that is "in harmony with the entirety of God's plan as

God himself has revealed it, and of which the mystery of the covenant (or the nuptial mystery) is the nucleus" (no. 5). In this view a priesthood of women would obscure at the symbolic level its immediate and perceivable christological reference and signification.

All in all, we can say that what matters theologically is the will of Christ as it has been interpreted by tradition; it is his to know the reasons why he has reserved the ministerial priesthood to men. This is not meant to imply an inferiority or humiliation of women, whose presence and work in the Church are absolutely necessary, although not ministerially.

8. The value of *Inter Insigniores* is that of having presented the method and theologically correct principles for removing the question of the ministerial priesthood from misleading approaches and references.

MARIAN PROFILE OF MINISTRY IS BASIS OF WOMAN'S ECCLESIAL ROLE

MAX THURIAN

The decision of the General Synod of the Church of England to ordain women to the ministry (11 November 1992) will not fail to create serious problems for ecumenical dialogue. Certainly the Anglican Communion is bound to experience new internal difficulties, and ecumenical solidarity demands an increase in our prayer and fraternal affection for so many Christian brothers and sisters who will suffer from this. The ecumenical movement has taught us, as Christians united by the sacrament of baptism, to share joys and trials. Even if it is difficult to understand this choice of the Church of England, the bonds between it and the Catholic Church continue to exist despite this recent decision regarding the ordination of women. Theological dialogue should continue, perhaps by deepening the concept of the priesthood. The official dialogue on ministry made us hope in a greater convergence perhaps than there really was (cf. ARCIC I).

It is clear that in recent years both sides have felt a great desire to rediscover the full dignity of woman and to use all of her potential in the area of the Church's mission and service (cf. John Paul II, *Mulieris Dignitatem*). Some have held that we ought to go so far as to admit women to the ordained ministry. One can say that the ecclesial communities lacked theological imagination in this case. There was the possibility of creating new ministries, suited to the nature and the gifts of woman. Why should we wish to ordain them to the "priesthood," which has assumed the form of a male service in the whole course of the Judeo-Christian biblical tradition, as well as throughout the entire history of the Church? To impose a male form of ministry on woman is to fail to respect her specific dignity. There are many ministries which would be far more consonant with woman's nature and talents.

Two Ministerial Profiles Exist in the Church

We might well ask here if there was not some confusion between the priesthood properly speaking, which conforms a man to Christ, the one and only priest, the bridegroom of the Church (cf. *Pastores Dabo Vobis*, nos. 12, 16), and the various forms which ministry took on in the ancient Church: prophecy, catechesis (*didascalia*), pastorate, diaconate. The ecclesial communities which accept the ordination of women to the ministry do not recognize a ministerial *priesthood* and they thus ordain to a ministerial *function* rather than to a priestly state. For the Catholic Church, the priest is in the Church and for the Church as a sacramental representation of Christ, the one high priest of the new and eternal covenant: he is a living and transparent image of Christ the priest. He is a derivation, a specific participation and an extension of Christ himself (*Pastores Dabo Vobis*, no. 12). For this reason, it is natural that as a "sacrament" of Christ the priest, the Catholic priest should correspond precisely with Christ himself, in his nature as man.

It should come as no surprise that non-Catholic ecclesial communities that do not have this sacramental conception of the priesthood accept the idea of ordaining women to the ministries of the word and of church leadership which do not imply a sacramental configuration to Christ in his whole person. This merely emphasizes the difference existing between the Catholic sacramental priesthood and non-Catholic ecclesial ministry.

One could speculate about ministries that would correspond to the nature and the charisms of woman and which could be of great service to the Church. One can say that there are two ministerial profiles in the Church: the apostolic and Petrine one, which stands at the origin of the sacramental priesthood of the presbyterate and the episcopate, and the Marian one of spiritual maternity, of contemplation and intercession (cf. Address of John Paul II to the Roman Curia, 22 Dec. 1987). It is to this Marian profile of the Church that we should look to discover in depth the role of woman in the Church and her possible ministry. "This link between the two profiles of the Church, the Marian and the Petrine, is therefore profound and complementary. This is so even though the

Marian profile is anterior not only in the design of God but also in time, as well as being supreme and pre-eminent, richer in personal and communitarian implications for individual ecclesial vocations" (Address to the Roman Curia, 22 Dec. 1987 no. 2, *L'Osservatore Romano* English-Language edition, 11 Jan. 1988, p. 6).

Catholic tradition is rich in all these forms of woman's ministry and the Holy Spirit could reveal others for the needs of our time.

How many nuns and women religious have exercised this ministry of spiritual motherhood, contemplation, and intercession! How many communities, how many secular institutes, how many movements today are discovering this ministry of woman, religious and lay, which, without being the sacramental priesthood, serves Christ and today's Church in the Marian line of ministry.

Spiritual Movements Offer New Possibilities

It is absolutely necessary to preserve and develop in the Church, which is a mother, the characteristic of femininity which is of her essence. To confer the ministerial priesthood on women would contradict their proper nature and the specific gifts which they possess. "By virtue of this consecration brought about by the outpouring of the Spirit in the sacrament of holy orders, the spiritual life of the priest is marked, molded, and characterized by the way of thinking and acting proper to Jesus Christ, Head and Shepherd of the Church, and which are summed up in his pastoral charity" (*Pastores Dabo Vobis,* no. 21). It is clear that the ministerial priesthood as it has been conceived for centuries does not conform to the proper nature of woman.

It is in the Marian nature of the Church, as virgin, bride, and mother, that the source of women's vocations and ministries in service to the Church should be sought.

It is rather striking to see how the ecclesial communities which are more orientated toward the pastoral consecration of women are those which have no experience, or only very limited experience, of the monastic or religious life. On the contrary, for the Catholic Church the monastic and religious life is an immense field in which the feminine ministries serving the Church flourish. Today the communities of modern foundation, the secular institutes, the spiritual movements at the heart of the Church are offering new possibilities for vocations and ministries in the Church to women, whether they are single or mothers of families.

In the light of the Marian nature of the Church as spiritual mother, vocations and ministries proper to women can be identified in great numbers in the Church. The ministry of woman is characterized by spiritual motherhood: gifts of acceptance, spiritual discernment, counseling, etc. The contemplative life and the spiritual combat of intercession are also among the specific gifts of the Christian woman who can be led to exercise a true ministry of leadership in the heart of the Church. Could not the catechetical ministry be further improved, and even the ministry of preaching on the part of women, not to mention teaching theology?

The coming synod on religious life will have an immense field for reflecting on how to develop all the potential of women's ministry in the Church as a complement to the ministerial priesthood of presbyters.

ORDINATION OF WOMEN CREATES
SERIOUS ECUMENICAL PROBLEMS

Jean Corbon

The decision made by the Synod of the Church of England on 11 November 1992 to allow the ordination of women to the priesthood does not come as a surprise to the Orthodox Churches. Such a decision is wholly within the logic of the Lambeth Conference (all the bishops of the Anglican Commission) which on 1 August 1988 had expressed itself with an overwhelming majority in favor of the ordination of women to the episcopate (423 votes in favor, 28 opposed, 19 abstaining).

One month earlier, the Mixed International Commission for theological dialogue between the Catholic Church and the Orthodox Church meeting at Uusi Valamo (Finland) had published its third joint document, entitled *The Sacrament of Order in the Sacramental Structure of the Church, with a Particular Reference to the Importance of the Apostolic Succession for the Sanctification and Unity of the People of God.*

In no. 32, the official representatives of the two Churches declared: "In the whole history of our Churches women have had a fundamental role witnessed to not only by the most holy Mother of God, but also by the holy women mentioned in the New Testament, by the numerous saints whom we venerate and by so many other women who right up till today have served the Church in numerous ways. Their specific charisms are very important for the building up of the body of Christ, but our Churches remain faithful to the historical and theological tradition according to which only men can be ordained to the priestly ministry" (cf. Pontifical Council for Promoting Christian Unity, *Information Service* 68 [1988], 197).

It should be noted that the problem of the ordination of women, which has been posed since 1897, had been discussed in the Lambeth Conferences of 1948 and 1978, and in 1988 about 1,200 women had

167

already been ordained to the priesthood in the various provinces of the Anglican Communion. The solid vote of 1 August 1988 in favor of the ordination of women to the episcopate dangerously shook one of the pillars of the "quadrilateral of Lambeth" on which the unity of the Anglican Communion rests ("the historical episcopate") and for this reason runs the risk of breaking one of its links of communion with the Catholic and Orthodox Churches.

Ordination of Women a Serious Ecumenical Problem

It is here that the ecumenical problem underlying the ordination of women is posed: in what pertains to the sacramental structure of the Church (baptism-confirmation, eucharist, and ordained ministry), or in what is essential to the faith handed down by the apostles, can a Church modify this structure on her own authority without compromising her communion with the other Churches of the same apostolic faith?

This is the precise point of the ecumenical problem which the representative of the Patriarch of Constantinople, the Metropolitan of Pergamum, Bishop John Zizioulas, stressed at Lambeth: "The fact that the Orthodox Church is decentralized is well known. . . . At the present moment a certain change of emphasis has begun to take place in this system that is autocephalous and of synodal practice. It is not a question of moving radically away from tradition, but rather of putting into practice the fundamental principles. The 'many' always have need of the 'one' in order to express themselves. This mystery of the 'one' and the 'many' is profoundly rooted in the theology of the Church, in its christological nature (the aspect of the 'one') and in its pneumatological nature (the aspect of the 'many'). At the institutional level there is an implicit presupposition of a ministry of primacy inherent in all the forms of conciliarity. An ecclesiology of communion, an ecclesiology which gives to the 'many' the right to be themselves runs the risk of a 'pneuma-tomonism,' if the ministry of the 'one' does not serve as a counter-balance. Likewise, the ecclesiology of a pyramidal hierarchical structure entails a christonomic tendency which can undermine the decisive role of the Holy Spirit in the life and structure of the Church. We must then find the golden mean, the correct balance between the 'one' and the 'many' and this, I fear, cannot be done unless we first seriously deepen our knowledge in the area of trinitarian theology. The God in whom we believe is 'one' while at the same time being 'many' (three) and is 'many' while at the same time being 'one.'

"The question of central authority in the Church is a question of faith and not only of constitution. A Church which is not capable of speaking with one voice is not the true image of the body of Christ.... A theology which justifies or even (as an Orthodox and perhaps also an Anglican might specify) necessitates an episcopal ministry at the level of the local Church—such a theology makes evident the need for a primacy at the regional and even at the universal level. It would be unfortunate if the Anglican Church were to go in an opposite direction. It would then have to seek a non-institutional type of identity and the result at the ecumenical level would be sad and perhaps even tragic.... Far from being an internal matter its unity is a question of vital interest for the whole Church....

Orthodox Acknowledge Missionary Work of Women

"It is no secret to anyone that the Orthodox are officially opposed to any decision of the Anglicans to ordain women to the priesthood, not to speak of the episcopate.... When there is such strong controversy the history of the ancient Church teaches us that no decision can be made before the disputed points have been subjected to an in-depth theological debate.... I think that at the ecumenical level we have not yet begun to treat the question of the ordination of women as a theological problem. Those who are opposed to the ordination of women have thus far advanced only reasons which pertain to the traditional practice, while those in favor are charged by their adversaries with having only sociological reasons. Before such a question is put to a vote it would perhaps be wise and more pertinent to the nature of the problem to debate the question theologically at the ecumenical level. What is there in the nature of priesthood that prohibits the ordination of women?

And what can necessitate the access of women to the priestly ministry, beyond the social reasons which are also serious and important?" (cf. *Service Orthodoxe de Presse*, 132 [1988], 20-22).

In order to find out where they stood on such questions, a meeting was held at Rhodes from 30 October to 7 November 1988, on the initiative of the ecumenical patriarch, to discuss "the position of woman in the Orthodox Church and the question of the ordination of women." In his message to the members of the congress, His Holiness Patriarch Dimitrios I recalled the fundamental data of the Orthodox tradition: "The growing authority of women in the historical evolution, the improvement of their social situation, and the recognition of their role in daily life depend on the revolutionary transformation and the institutional reform of the ancient world promoted by Christianity. Our Lord Jesus Christ did not go along with the historical conditions of his time, nor with the social conventions hostile to women. . . . We are certain that the missionary activity of women in the era of Christ and the apostles and also, thereafter, in the earliest Christian communities, was contrary to the customs of the time. . . .

"Following the example of the Lord and of the apostles, the Church in her history throughout the ages has recruited men and women without discrimination. In her struggle for salvation and spiritual perfection, she has never engaged in any kind of discrimination. The Orthodox Church accepts with benevolence the participation of woman in social life where, very often, the feminine element proves to be superior to male activity. This Church, moreover, maintains that the achievements of women are an application of the religious freedom on which any healthy feminist movement should be based.

"Nevertheless, the effort toward equality when pushed beyond its limits creates insurmountable obstacles for the union of Christians, so much desired and sought, and accordingly does not have a place in the Church of Christ. In fact such an effort seeks not only to level the biological differences between the two sexes, but also to extend the feminist claims even to the sphere of the mystery of salvation and the Church, and all this, in particular, with the problem recently raised by the admission of women to the priesthood.

"We would like to hope that the inter-Orthodox congress of Rhodes can contribute positively to clarifying and interpreting the theological reasons why the Orthodox Church believes that the ordination of women is impossible. It is not a matter of mere rhetoric, but of an attitude firmly founded on sacred Tradition and historical reality. Can the Church really have been in error during all these centuries in denying the priesthood to women? Not only was the Church not in error, but she condemned with full consciousness those who advanced such claims. The catholicity of the Church is not only geographical, it traverses time as well. This means that the Church guards that which has been entrusted to her in the course of the centuries. She guards 'that which has been believed everywhere, always, and by all'" (cf. *Episkepsis, 409 [1988]* 5-7).

Eastern Orthodox Share Common Ecclesiological Principles

The participants in this inter-Orthodox theological congress represented all the Orthodox Churches in communion with the Ecumenical See of Constantinople. They included clerics and lay people, monks and nuns, men and women. In its final statement "the congress acknowledges that the Orthodox woman is capable of living the life of the Church fully and of exercising the ecclesial service suitable to her both inside and outside of the Church in diverse forms always of an ecclesial nature, but not priestly. Invested with the dignity and position of deaconess, a most ancient institution of the Orthodox Church, and together with other functions, the Orthodox woman is called today to participate in the Church's mission in sectors such as the apostolate, liturgical service, catechesis, teaching, mission, social service, in addition to her presence and her specific contribution of monasticism" (ibid., 3).

In reading the detailed and reasoned conclusion of this congress, the first in the history of the Orthodox Church, it is impossible not to note the convergence in ecclesiological and sacramental principles which are common to the Eastern Orthodox Churches (Armenian, Coptic, Ethiopian, Syrian of Antioch and of India). In these conclusions one can also note the sincere recognition of the fact that the Christian communities have not always been faithful, in practice, to the principle of the equal dignity of woman and man in the life of the Church. There is a further convergence in the discernment of the motives behind the modern feminist movement which, under the appearance of theological formulations, are often in fact raising socio-cultural questions. This would make it possible to clarify the ambiguity of the Anglican position whose reformed element, as is well known, does not recognize the ordained ministry as sacramental. Finally, one will note the move made by the Congress of Rhodes to restore the female diaconate, without fearing to see in this a first step toward the priesthood, because in this sacrament, and according to the most ancient tradition, the imposition of hands is received "not in view of priesthood, but of ministry" (cf. *Lumen Gentium*, no. 29 and note 74. The conclusions of the Inter-Orthodox Theological Congress of Rhodes have been published in *Episkepsis*, 412 [1989], 8-17).

WOMAN'S SPIRITUAL MOTHERHOOD ATTESTS TO GOD'S MERCY AND LOVE

JUTTA BURGGRAF

"Before I formed you in the womb I knew you, before you were born I dedicated you" (Jer 1:5). God speaks with clarity to his prophet, and his words could be directed to every one of us: it is he who gives life and, when he desires the birth of a new human being, it is he who has a wonderful design for the child, deeply rooted in his eternal plan.

Why do these ideas trouble us so much today? Do we perhaps fear that our freedom might be threatened, our self-fulfillment hindered or our "dignity" limited, if we are unable to "plan ourselves," to "make ourselves" what we want to be—and instead we feel indebted to someone other than ourselves? Perhaps in these fears we have unconsciously yielded to the depressing and destructive influence of atheistic existentialism. In fact, for a Christian, it ought to be a joy that we are known and understood by the good God even to the depths of our being, loved in all the circumstances of life and thus taken with radical seriousness. For each of us, considered in our individuality, the Creator has a particular design; he is counting on each of us for the realization of his plans, and he invites each of us to follow his call. If only we had the courage really to abandon ourselves to him, we would walk more happily through life; we could develop harmoniously within the "immeasurable" love of God, and our lives would acquire ultimate meaning.

It is generally known that no one exists as a human being *per se*, but only as male or female. From the first moment of our existence the sexual difference is established. It is not something accessory or supplementary, nor a mere circumstance, which need not be present. Carefully considered, it appears as an expression of the divine will to see human existence realized in two reciprocally correlative and complementary expressions. God must have had a precise intention if he did not create man androgynous. A parthenogenetic or a totally asexual form of propagation, or other possibilities corresponding to the many types of relations found in the animal world, could be imagined.

Man and Woman Are Distinguished "Ontologically"

Nor does "woman" as such exist, but only "this concrete woman" with her nature and her history, her social milieu and her talents, her strong points and her weaknesses. This explains the tendency toward the multiplicity and diversity of tasks in the family, in the Church, in society. If in what follows we prescind now and then from all personal characteristics, we do so consciously in order to bring to light the root of "being woman." This procedure is obviously risky, and in some cases it can certainly miss the mark. Nevertheless, within the context of a personal reflection it does not seem totally inappropriate, considering how heatedly people throughout the world are discussing the question of "emancipation."

What does it mean to be "male" or "female"? How are the sexes distinguished? Unfortunately, not all the answers given to this question throughout the history of humanity have been intelligent and constructive. Sometimes the man has been ridiculed in summary, superficial judgments; other times (and, to tell the truth, much more often) the tendency has been to lock woman into a narrow stereotype, humiliating her in theory and in practice. In fact each of the sexes has its specific qualities; moreover, each in its own sphere is superior to the other. Man and woman are not distinguished by the level of their respective intellectual or moral qualities, but rather by a much more profound, more "ontological" consideration: namely, the capacity to be a father or a mother, and the special gifts that derive from this.

Woman is called to motherhood. The debate that has arisen in recent decades over this self-evident factual datum is surprising. Some radical feminists see motherhood as a "sickness," a "threat," a "shackle of nature," from which the emancipated woman should free herself. Many women are unaware of how greatly they are influenced by this perspective, how much their own scale of values depends on it in regard to "self-fulfillment," the number of children, and salaried employment. Nevertheless, an ever increasing number of Christians are managing to escape this cultural terrorism. To the extent that they enjoy an ever deepening experience of faith, they understand that rebellion against their own nature means rebelling against the Creator—and that one can have a balanced personality only by living at peace with oneself and one's body. The "self-liberation" of woman cannot be reduced to a banal leveling according to the male model. One must aim at something much more challenging, much more fruitful, but also much more difficult: woman's acceptance of her diversity, of her singularity as woman.

As mother, woman is called to be the "locus" of a divine creative act; in fact, whenever a new human being is born, parents cooperate in an indescribable way with God. The child is entrusted to the woman even before it is entrusted to the man; it is she who will welcome (above all in her very self), guard, and nourish it. To be sure, pregnancy is often characterized by tiredness and exhaustion, but is this not perhaps a special honor for woman, allowing her to feel the creative love of God even in the innermost depths of her body? Only a very superficial perspective, one which has lost its sensitivity to the essentials of life, can claim that a woman is lessened or put at disadvantage by being a mother. The Christian viewpoint holds the exact opposite: precisely because of her motherhood, woman possesses a certain "precedence over man," as John Paul II expressed it so delicately (*Mulieris Dignitatem*, no. 19).

Woman Cooperates Actively in Spreading God's Kingdom

This does not mean that the mother is "bound to the house as if by a chain," "condemned to the work of a slave," even if for some time feminist circles have held that this is obviously true. The fact is that many women experience the birth of a child as a burden—a fact which can in part depend on the lack of understanding from others and in part also on unjust social structures. Nevertheless, these are consequences of sin, not circumstances intrinsic to motherhood. Therefore they can never justify denying life to a new human being; rather, these circumstances themselves should be eliminated! This is one of the most urgent challenges in all societies precisely for Christians.

When a woman consents to be a mother, then she is able to follow Christ in a more interior though probably unspectacular way. She can testify to the "kindness and love of God" (Ti 3:4) by offering a welcoming home, providing hospitality, handing on cultural and religious values. Thus she will learn that Christ can be found only on the cross. Undoubtedly she will also discover that she is called by her position to cooperate actively in spreading the kingdom of God. For this reason it is not at all desirable for her to be "confined" within four walls. Depending on her own personal ability and her family situation, she can actually consider it her duty also to seek other forms of involvement in society (professional, volunteer, or even personal engagement) and to open her home to many persons. However, it is undeniable that the welfare of the family must always be the first concern of good parents.

Motherhood, moreover, cannot be reduced to the physical realm. From the psychological-spiritual viewpoint all women are called in some way to be "mother." What does it actually mean to be a mother if not to break through people's anonymity, to offer others a willing ear, to share their concerns—and to make them open to the grace of God? Normally this all comes naturally to a woman (if she has not been subjected to distorting influences); her capacity to size up concrete situations, her sense of reality, and her sensitivity to the spiritual needs of others can be of great help to her. She has received from her Creator the capacity for solidarity and friendship and for a more personalized transmission of the faith. Why should one deny these gifts rather than use them gratefully and make life more agreeable and more in accord with the will of God? "Whenever a person realizes," Blessed Edith Stein points out, "that in the workplace, where everyone runs the risk of becoming a cog in a great machine, there await him a sharing and even a willingness to help, then in his heart much of what otherwise would have wilted can be kept alive or rekindled."

Here we can see so clearly what great good a Christian can do in the world! Is it not a highly significant mission to create an environment in which people can feel at ease? Precisely as a Christian, woman has the supremely important task of bearing witness to God's love for the individual. She is called to convey to others the awareness that they are accepted and taken seriously (by God too), and that their life has value. To be Christian means to live in union with Christ and to act as he would, even amid the hectic pace of the big city, in the supermarket and in the factory, in the office and in the university, in the hospital and in Parliament, and above all at home, at work, in sports and recreation. It means showing that there is someone to whom a person can turn when problems become too great, someone who does not judge or pose as an expert, but understands, forgives, and comforts, and who asks more of herself than of others.

Spiritual Motherhood Brings Happiness and Love

The "Church" is to be found wherever a human person follows Christ, even without an explicit mission or the presence of a parish council. A woman who takes her ecclesial mission in the world seriously has an almost unlimited panorama before her. There is no sorrow or need which can leave her indifferent because she knows the state of the world, but at the same time she always experiences that peace which comes from faith. Through the example of her life she will proclaim the joyful message, whose demands should shake and confound all near-sighted selfishness. Acting in a Christian way means to act humanely; it means to work with magnanimity and untarnished fidelity, as much for the present world as for the world to come.

Women who spend themselves in a spiritual motherhood are usually very happy and very much loved. There is no sense in trying to alert them to the fact that they may be "exploited." If Christ died for mankind, then those who follow him cannot afford to be concerned with the narrow calculation of their own advantage—which on the other hand leads only to neurotic benumbing and sadness. We continually have to learn to repent of our own hardness of heart and to change our lives; then we will experience the joy of a new beginning.

The silent but effective work of "motherhood" deepens and broadens the Church's life all over the world. It is not triumphs and external splendor that constitutes what is essential in the Church of Christ; it is not careers or production. It is certainly not status or position. Much more important is a personal, strong, interior union with Christ himself. More important is the love of God which is expressed in love of human beings. Women are called to be an enduring reminder of this truth.

Does this perhaps mean that men are incapable of love and friendship? Certainly not! Fortunately, the opposite often proves to be true. However, since by his very nature man is more remote from concrete life, he can and should learn much from women—first of all from his mother, and then from his sisters, his women friends, his wife, and his coworkers.

On the other hand, women are not prevented from holding office or receiving appointments—even in the Church's institutions. Here they are not inferior to lay males, and they have amply demonstrated that they too have the capacity to organize and manage. However, in God's sight this is secondary. A woman who wishes to be faithful to herself and to Christ will in any case desire an authoritative position only in order to be better able to spend herself for the happiness of others. And she will never forget that it is holiness which confers value on a human being—not the world's acclaim.

WOMEN ARE CALLED TO BEAR CHRIST INTO THEIR FAMILIES AND THE WORLD

Joyce Little

It is to all practical intents and purposes impossible to speak in a Catholic way about the advancement of women within the context of the feminist debate, inasmuch as the feminist notion of advancement is tied to inadequate or false notions of faith, freedom, and authority. From the feminist point of view, faith arises out of and is defined by the experience of women, freedom is linked to liberation from the realities and responsibilities of marriage and childbearing (as in "reproductive freedom"), and authority is viewed solely as power. Hence feminists seek "empowerment," and see women's ordination as the means for getting a place in the power structure of the Catholic Church.

Does this mean that there is no truth at all in the feminist challenge to the Catholic Church? Not at all. The feminists are a constant reminder to us of inadequacies in some traditional Catholic conceptions not only regarding women, but regarding the importance of the female character of the new covenant established by Christ. The new covenant, as Pope John Paul II has pointed out, was inaugurated by Mary at the annunciation (*Redemptoris Missio*, no. 27) and consists ultimately of the marital union of Christ and the Church (Eph 5:32). Jesus Christ is the sole mediator of the new covenant. But the new covenant involves a relationship of reciprocity and interdependence of Jesus Christ with Mary in his earthly ministry and with the Church after his ascension. Both Mary and the Church are charged with bearing Christ into the world. The relationship of Christ to Church as vine to branches (Jn 15) makes it clear that while there can be no Church without Christ, there also can be no effective presence of Christ in the world without the Church (since it is the branches, not the vine, which bear the fruit). The advancement of women, therefore, depends upon a proper reading of the Christ/Church relationship and is irrevocably linked to the Marian/ecclesial side of the new covenant and of the Catholic faith.

Cause of Women Not Served by Rejecting Catholic Faith

This means, first, that the true advancement of women rests upon a true understanding of the faith of the Church. The cause of women is not well served either by the feminist repudiation of traditional Catholic faith or by inadequate theologies of the Catholic faith which fail to take into account the enormous significance of the Marian/ecclesial character of the new covenant. To repudiate or to misunderstand the faith of the Church is to repudiate or to misunderstand the female role of Mary and the Church in relationship to the male role of Jesus Christ within that covenant.

Nothing could be clearer in the revelation given to us than that the sexual differentiation of male and female is created by God and constitutes a part of the good creation. Indeed, it is precisely as male and female that we image God (Gn 1:27). That this sexual differentiation is bound up with marital union is equally clear (Gn 2:24), but what is most striking is that sexual differentiation and marital union have as their ultimate goal the marital union of Christ and the Church (Eph 5:31-32). Creation is ordered from the outset to the covenantal, marital union of Christ and the Church. The advancement of women (and of men as well) depends upon our understanding these most basic facts of God's good creation and of the new covenant. The first intimation we are given of the character of the differentiation between male and female comes after the fall, in the so-called curses meted out to Adam and Eve (Gn 3:16-19). Each is hurt by the fall in different ways which reveal to us the specific roles and vulnerabilities of each. Adam is hurt in his relationship to his work and to the world around him. Eve is hurt in her relationships to Adam and to the children she will bear. If the specifically male sphere is defined by work and by the world, the specific female sphere is defined by marriage, home, and family. Although we are told to call no man father (Mt 23:9), Eve is "mother of all the living" (Gn 3:20), Mary is the Mother of God, and the Church is the mother of all the children of God. Because every woman is defined in her being as mother, "God entrusts the human being to her in a special way" *(Mulieris Dignitatem, no. 30).*

It is tragic that so many people, including so many feminists, regard the identification of women with home, marriage, family, and personal relationships as demeaning to women. The current pontiff has said that women have a special priority in the "order of love" *(Mulieris Dignitatem, no. 29).* There can be nothing demeaning about this when we consider that God is love. Pope John Paul II has also said that "the future of humanity passes by way of the family" *(Familiaris Consortio, no. 86).* Therefore, women, in the Catholic view of things, stand not on the periphery but at the very center of the reality of both creation and redemption.

The advancement of women is connected to the health of marriage, of family, of personal relationships. There can be no advancement of women (or anyone else) in a society in which those realities are unhealthy or disintegrating, as they so clearly are today in Western societies. Women are, therefore, called to place the well-being of marriage, family, and personal relationships at the center of their lives and concerns.

Third, it is the specific female role of Mary and the Church to bear Christ into the world. Although it is not much commented upon, in the context of the laity (whether male or female) in the Church the female role of making salvation a reality in the whole of creation is essential. The primary vocation of the laity does not lie, as so many lay people today seem to think, in service to the local parish, however important such service might be. The special obligation of the laity, as Vatican II pointed out, is the renewal of the temporal order *(Apostolicam Actuositatem, no. 7).* Pope John Paul II affirms this, reminding us that the laity are called to "consecrate the world itself to God" *(Familiaris Consortio, no. 56).*

Women Are Called to Bear Christ

Women in particular are called to bear Christ, first, into their families, bringing up children who are the sons and daughters of God, and second, into the larger world, by living out and bearing witness to the order of love, in which the sacred values of human life and personhood from the moment of conception to the moment of natural death are placed ahead of the secular values of power, fame, and fortune.

As regards these secular values, it should be noted, finally, that nothing is more misinformed than the feminist notion that the priesthood will give women access to power in the Church. The magisterium exercises not *power* but *authority*, and there is a world of difference between the two. Power is the exercise of the human will over reality, to change or affect it in some way. Authority is the ability to discern a reality and to define the doctrines of the faith. The magisterium has no power to change the reality of revelation. The magisterium has only the authority to discern the mind of Christ and the truth as Christ embodies and reveals it. The notion that the pope and/or the bishops could allow divorce and remarriage, contraception, the ordination of women, and a host of other things desired today rests upon the assumption that they exercise power, not authority. But they have no power to change what Christ has revealed. They have only the authority to discern that revelation. The pope and the bishops are as bound to the faith of the Church as is every other member of the Church. This is what Hans Urs von Balthasar meant when he said that "the feminine, Marian principle is, in the Church, what encompasses all other principles, even the Petrine" (in the epilogue to Louis Bouyer, *Women in the Church*, trans. Marilyn Teichert [San Francisco: Ignatius Press, 1979], p. 113).

Thus do we come full circle. Everything in our lives as Catholics, male and female alike, depends upon the feminine, Marian faith of the Church. To destroy that faith renders all else, including the authority of the magisterium, null and void. All of us therefore have an obligation to know our faith, defend it, insist that our bishops and priests preach it in and out of season, and, most important of all, live it and, in so doing, make it the leaven by which the whole of the temporal order is consecrated to God.

EPISTOLA APOSTOLICA

DE SACERDOTALI ORDINATIONE
VIRIS TANTUM RESERVANDA

Venerabiles Fratres in episcopatu!

1. Ordinatio sacerdotalis, per quam munus traditur, quod Christus Apostolis suis concredidit fideles docendi, sanctificandi et regendi, in Ecclesia Catholica inde ab initio semper solis viris reservata est. Quam traditionem Ecclesiae etiam Orientales fideliter retinuerunt.

Quando quaestio orta est de ordinatione mulierum apud Communionem Anglicanam, Summus Pontifex Paulus VI, pro sua fidelitate erga officium custodiendi Traditionem apostolicam, atque etiam ut novum impedimentum positum in itinere ad unitatem christianorum amoveret, fratres Anglicanos commonefecit de Ecclesiae Catholicae positione: « Ipsa retinet non esse admittendam ordinationem mulierum ad sacerdotium ob rationes fundamentales. Quae rationes complectuntur: exemplum Christi in Sacra Scriptura memoratum, qui tantummodo inter viros elegit suos Apostolos; constantem Ecclesiae usum, quae Christum imitata est in solis viris eligendis; eiusque vivum magisterium, quod congruenter statuit mulierum exclusionem a sacerdotio convenire cum consilio Dei pro sua Ecclesia ».[1]

---

[1] Cf PAULUS VI, *Rescriptum ad litteras Suae Gratiae Rev.mi Doctoris F. D. Coogan, Archiepiscopi Cantuariensis, de sacerdotali mulierum ministerio*, die 30 mensis Novembris anno 1975: AAS 68 (1976) 599-600: « Your Grace is of course well aware of the Catholic Church's position on this question. She holds that it is not admissible to ordain women to the priesthood, for very fundamental reasons. These reasons include: the example recorded in the Sacred Scriptures of Christ choosing his Apostles only from among men; the constant practice of the Church, which has imitated Christ in choosing only men; and her living teaching authority which has consistently held that the exclusion of women from the priesthood is in accordance with the God's plan for his Church » (p. 599).

APOSTOLIC LETTER ON RESERVING
PRIESTLY ORDINATION TO MEN ALONE

Venerable brothers in the episcopate:

1. Priestly ordination, which hands on the office entrusted by Christ to his apostles of teaching, sanctifying, and governing the faithful, has in the Catholic Church from the beginning always been reserved to men alone. This tradition has also been faithfully maintained by the Oriental churches.

When the question of the ordination of women arose in the Anglican Communion, Pope Paul VI, out of fidelity to his office of safeguarding the apostolic tradition, and also with a view to removing a new obstacle placed in the way of Christian unity, reminded Anglicans of the position of the Catholic Church:

"She holds that it is not admissible to ordain women to the priesthood, for very fundamental reasons. These reasons include the example recorded in the sacred scriptures of Christ choosing his apostles only from among men; the constant practice of the Church, which has imitated Christ in choosing only men; and her living teaching authority which has consistently held that the exclusion of women from the priesthood is in accordance with God's plan for his church."[1]

But since the question had also become the subject of debate among theologians and in certain Catholic circles, Paul VI directed the Congregation for the Doctrine of the Faith to set forth and expound the teaching of the Church on this matter. This was done through the dec-

---

[1] Paul VI, response to the letter of Rev. Dr. F. D. Coggan, Archbishop of Canterbury, concerning the ordination of women to the priesthood (Nov. 30, 1975): *AAS, 68* (1976), 599.

Cum tamen etiam inter theologos atque in aliquibus catholicis circulis quaestio in controversiam deducta esset, Paulus VI Congregationi pro Doctrina Fidei mandavit ut de hoc argumento Ecclesiae doctrinam exponeret atque illustraret. Quod factum est per Declarationem *Inter insigniores*, quam ipse Summus Pontifex approbavit et publici iuris fieri iussit.[2]

2. Quae quidem Declaratio huius doctrinae rationes fundamentales, a Paulo VI propositas, repetit et explicat, atque concludit Ecclesiam « auctoritatem sibi non agnoscere admittendi mulieres ad sacerdotalem ordinationem ».[3] Talibus rationibus fundamentalibus idem documentum alias addit rationes theologicas quibus convenientia illustratur illius consilii divini, et etiam aperte ostendit Christi agendi modum non ex causis sociologicis vel culturalibus, illius aetatis propriis, proficisci. Sicut deinde Paulus VI explicavit, « ratio vera in eo est, quod Christus, Ecclesiam propria fundamentali constitutione propriaque anthropologia theologica instruendo, sic statuit, quam deinceps eiusdem Ecclesiae Traditio semper observavit ».[4]

In Epistola Apostolica *Mulieris dignitatem* Nos Ipsi de hac materia scripsimus: « Advocans solos viros uti Apostolos suos Christus sese ratione gessit prorsus libera suique iuris. Eadem istud libertate fecit, qua toto in vitae suae instituto dignitatem extulit mulieris vocationemque, non tamen accommodans se vigentibus moribus ac traditionibus lege illius temporis constitutis ».[5]

Evangelia enim et Actus Apostolorum testificantur hanc vocationem factam esse secundum aeternum Dei consilium: Christus elegit quos voluit ipse (cf *Mc* 3,13-14; *Io* 6,70), idque fecit una cum Patre, « per Spiritum Sanctum » (*Act* 1,2), postquam pernoctaverat in ora-

---

[2] Cf Congregatio pro Doctrina Fidei, Declaratio *Inter insigniores* quoad admissionem mulierum ad sacerdotium ministeriale, die 15 mensis Octobris anno 1976: AAS 69 (1977) 98-116.

[3] *Ibid.*, 100.

[4] Paulus VI, Allocutio *Il ruolo della donna nel disegno della salvezza*, die 30 mensis Ianuarii anno 1977: *Insegnamenti*, vol. XV (1977) 111. Cf etiam Ioannes Paulus II, Adhortatio Apostolica *Christifideles laici*, die 30 mensis Decembris anno 1988, n. 51: AAS 81 (1989) 492-496; *Catéchisme de l'Église Catholique*, n. 1577.

[5] Epistola Apostolica *Mulieris dignitatem*, die 15 mensis Augusti anno 1988, n. 26: AAS 80 (1988) 1715.

laration *Inter Insigniores*, which the supreme pontiff approved and ordered to be published.[2]

2. The declaration recalls and explains the fundamental reasons for this teaching, reasons expounded by Paul VI, and concludes that the Church "does not consider herself authorized to admit women to priestly ordination."[3] To these fundamental reasons the document adds other theological reasons which illustrate the appropriateness of the divine provision, and it also shows clearly that Christ's way of acting did not proceed from sociological or cultural motives peculiar to his time. As Paul VI later explained: 'The real reason is that, in giving the Church her fundamental constitution, her theological anthropology— thereafter always followed by the Church's tradition—Christ established things in this way."[4]

In the apostolic letter *Mulieris Dignitatem*, I myself wrote in this regard:

"In calling only men as his apostles, Christ acted in a completely free and sovereign manner. In doing so, he exercised the same freedom with which, in all his behavior, he emphasized the dignity and the vocation of women, without conforming to the prevailing customs and to the traditions sanctioned by the legislation of the time."[5]

In fact, the Gospels and the Acts of the Apostles attest that this call was made in accordance with God's eternal plan: Christ chose those whom he willed (cf. Mk 3:13-14; Jn 6:70), and he did so in union with the Father, "through the Holy Spirit" (Acts 1:2), after having spent the night in prayer (cf. Lk 6:12). Therefore, in granting admission to the

---

[2] Cf. Congregation for the Doctrine of the Faith, declaration *Inter Insigniores* on the question of the admission of women to the ministerial priesthood (Oct. 15, 1976): *AAS,* 69 (1977), 98-116.

[3] Ibid, p. 100.

[4] Paul VI, address on the role of women in the plan of salvation (Jan. 30, 1977): *Insegnamenti*, XV (1977), 111. Cf. also John Paul II, apostolic exhortation *Christifideles Laici* (Dec. 30, 1988), 51: *AAS*, 81 (1989), 393-521; *Catechism of the Catholic Church*, 1577.

[5] Apostolic letter *Mulieris Dignitatem* (Aug. 15, 1988), 26: *AAS*, 80 (1988), 1715.

tione (cf *Lc* 6,12). Quapropter in admissione ad sacerdotium ministeriale,[6] Ecclesia semper tamquam constantem normam agnovit Domini sui agendi rationem in duodecim virorum electione, quos Ipse posuit Ecclesiae suae fundamentum (cf *Apc* 21,14). Qui quidem non tantum munus acceperunt, quod deinde a quolibet Ecclesiae membro exerceri potuisset, sed iidem peculiariter et arte cum ipsius Verbi Incarnati missione sunt consociati (cf *Mt* 10,1.7-8; 28,16-20; *Mc* 3,13-16; 16,14-15). Apostoli idem fecerunt cum cooperatores suos elegerunt,[7] qui ipsis successuri erant in ministerio.[8] Qua in electione illi quoque inclusi erant qui, decursu temporum Ecclesiae, ipsorum Apostolorum munus prosequerentur, scilicet vicem gerendi Christi Domini ac Redemptoris.[9]

3. Ceterum, quod Maria Sanctissima, Dei et Ecclesiae Mater, munus non accepit Apostolorum proprium, neque sacerdotium ministeriale, clare ostendit non admissionem mulierum ad sacerdotalem ordinationem non posse minorem earum dignitatem significare nec discrimen erga eas, sed fidelem observantiam consilii, quod sapientiae Domini universi est tribuendum.

Mulieris praesentia eiusque in Ecclesiae vita missioneque partes, etsi non sunt cum sacerdotio ministeriali coniunctae, perstant tamen ratione absoluta necessariae et eae quae substitui non possint. Sicut sane ipsa illustrat Declaratio *Inter insigniores*, « exoptat sancta Mater Ecclesia, ut christianae mulieres sibi plene consciae fiant, quanta sit ipsarum missio: partes earum hodie maximae sunt, ut simul et instauretur atque humanior fiat societas et fideles veram Ecclesiae imaginem agnoscant ».[10] Novum Testamentum cunctaque Ecclesiae historia satis superque testantur in Ecclesia praesentiam mulierum germanarum discipularum et testium Christi in familia atque in civili professione praeter quam in integra dedicatione famulatui Dei et Evangelii. « Mulieris dignitatem tutando Ecclesia eiusque vocationem

---

[6] Cf Constitutio dogmatica *Lumen gentium*, n. 28; decretum *Presbyterorum Ordinis*, n. 2b.

[7] Cf *1 Tim* 3,1-13; *2 Tim* 1,6; *Tit* 1,5-9.

[8] Cf *Catéchisme de l'Église Catholique*, n. 1577.

[9] Cf Constitutio dogmatica *Lumen gentium*, n. 20 et n. 21.

[10] Congregatio pro Doctrina Fidei, Declaratio *Inter insigniores*, VI: AAS 69 (1977) 115-116.

ministerial priesthood,[6] the Church has always acknowledged as a perennial norm her Lord's way of acting in choosing the twelve men whom he made the foundation of his Church (cf. Rv 21:14). These men did not in fact receive only a function which could thereafter be exercised by any member of the Church; rather they were specifically and intimately associated in the mission of the incarnate Word himself (cf. Mt 10:1, 7-8; 28:16-20; Mk 3:13-16; 16:14-15). The apostles did the same when they chose fellow workers[7] who would succeed them in their ministry.[8] Also included in this choice were those who, throughout the time of the Church, would carry on the apostles' mission of representing Christ the Lord and Redeemer.[9]

3. Furthermore, the fact that the Blessed Virgin Mary, mother of God and mother of the Church, received neither the mission proper to the apostles nor the ministerial priesthood clearly shows that the nonadmission of women to priestly ordination cannot mean that women are of lesser dignity nor can it be construed as discrimination against them. Rather, it is to be seen as the faithful observance of a plan to be ascribed to the wisdom of the Lord of the universe.

The presence and the role of women in the life and mission of the Church, although not linked to the ministerial priesthood, remain absolutely necessary and irreplaceable. As the declaration *Inter Insigniores* points out, "the Church desires that Christian women should become fully aware of the greatness of their mission: Today their role is of capital importance both for the renewal and humanization of society and for the rediscovery by believers of the true face of the Church."[10] The New Testament and the whole history of the Church give ample evidence of the presence in the Church of women, true disciples, witnesses to Christ in the family and in society, as well as in total consecration to the service of God and of the Gospel. "By defending the dignity

---

[6] Cf. Dogmatic constitution *Lumen Gentium*, 28; decree *Presbyterorum Ordinis*, 2b.

[7] Cf. 1 Tm 3:1-13; 2 Tm 1:6; Ti 1:5-9.

[8] Cf. *Catechism*, 1577.

[9] Cf. *Lumen Gentium*, 20, 21.

[10] *Inter Insigniores*, 6.

honorem tribuit atque gratias iis quae, Evangelio fideles, omni aetate apostolicum communicarunt totius Dei Populi munus. De martyribus sanctis agitur et de virginibus ac de matribus familias fortiter quae fidem sunt testificatae ac suis educandis liberis in Evangelii principiis fidem tradiderunt Ecclesiaeque traditionem ».[11]

Ceterum ad fidelium sanctitatem funditus ordinatur hierarchica Ecclesiae constitutio. Ideo memorat Declaratio *Inter insigniores*, « unum charisma melius, quod quis aemulari potest ac debet, est caritas (cf *1 Cor* 12-13). Maiores in Regno caelorum non sunt ministri, sed sancti ».[12]

4. Quamvis doctrina de ordinatione sacerdotali viris tantum reservanda constanti et universali Ecclesiae Traditione servetur atque Magisterio in recentioribus documentis firmiter doceatur, temporibus tamen nostris diversis in partibus disputabilis habetur, aut etiam Ecclesiae sententiae non admittendi mulieres ad ordinationem illam vis mere disciplinaris tribuitur.

Ut igitur omne dubium auferatur circa rem magni momenti, quae ad ipsam Ecclesiae divinam constitutionem pertinet, virtute ministerii Nostri confirmandi fratres (cf *Lc* 22,32), declaramus Ecclesiam facultatem nullatenus habere ordinationem sacerdotalem mulieribus conferendi, hancque sententiam ab omnibus Ecclesiae fidelibus esse definitive tenendam.

In vos omnes, Venerabiles Fratres, atque in omnem Christianum populum implorantes perpetuum divinum praesidium, libentes quidem omnibus Apostolicam Benedictionem impertimus.

Ex Aedibus Vaticanis, die XXII mensis Maii, in Sollemnitate Pentecostes, anno MCMXCIV, sexto decimo Pontificatus Nostri.

IOANNES PAULUS PP. II

---

[11] IOANNES PAULUS II, Epistola Apostolica *Mulieris dignitatem*, n. 27: AAS 80 (1988) 1719.
[12] CONGREGATIO PRO DOCTRINA FIDEI, Declaratio *Inter insigniores*, VI: AAS 69 (1977) 115.

of women and their vocation, the church has shown honor and gratitude for those women who—faithful to the Gospel—have shared in every age in the apostolic mission of the whole people of God. They are the holy martyrs, virgins, and the mothers of families, who bravely bore witness to their faith and passed on the Church's faith and tradition by bringing up their children in the spirit of the Gospel."[11]

Moreover, it is to the holiness of the faithful that the hierarchical structure of the Church is totally ordered. For this reason, the declaration *Inter Insigniores* recalls: "The only better gift, which can and must be desired, is love (cf. 1 Cor 12 and 13). The greatest in the kingdom of heaven are not the ministers but the saints."[12]

4. Although the teaching that priestly ordination is to be reserved to men alone has been preserved by the constant and universal tradition of the Church and firmly taught by the magisterium in its more recent documents, at the present time in some places it is nonetheless considered still open to debate, or the Church's judgment that women are not to be admitted to ordination is considered to have a merely disciplinary force.

Wherefore, in order that all doubt may be removed regarding a matter of great importance, a matter which pertains to the Church's divine constitution itself, in virtue of my ministry of confirming the brethren (cf. Lk 22:32) I declare that the Church has no authority whatsoever to confer priestly ordination on women and that this judgment is to be definitively held by all the Church's faithful.

Invoking an abundance of divine assistance upon you, venerable brothers, and upon all the faithful, I impart my apostolic blessing.

From the Vatican, on May 22, the solemnity of Pentecost, in the year 1994, the 16th of my pontificate.

JOHN PAUL II

---

[11] *Mulieris Dignitatem*, 27.
[12] *Inter Insigniores*, 6.

AN OVERVIEW OF THE APOSTOLIC LETTER

With the apostolic letter *Ordinatio Sacerdotalis*, dated May 22, the solemnity of Pentecost, the supreme pontiff Pope John Paul II expressly intends to fulfill his office as successor of Peter, confirming by virtue of his apostolic ministry the teaching according to which the Church does not have the authority to confer priestly ordination on women, and declaring that this teaching is to be definitively held by all the faithful.

In particular, the Holy Father recalls that this teaching, based on the Church's constant and universal tradition, which from the beginning has reserved priestly ordination to men, had been authoritatively presented and explained by the Congregation for the Doctrine of the Faith in its declaration *Inter Insigniores* on the question of the admission of women to the ministerial priesthood, published on Oct. 15, 1976, by order of Pope Paul VI and with his approval.

Referring to that declaration, the supreme pontiff calls attention to the fundamental reasons why the Church is aware that she does not have the authority to admit women to priestly ordination: They are to be found in the example of Christ who chose the twelve apostles from among men, in the apostolic tradition, and in the constant magisterium of the Church. The present letter also mentions the other recent documents of the magisterium which repeat the same teaching: the apostolic letter *Mulieris Dignitatem* (no. 26), the postsynodal apostolic exhortation *Christifideles Laici* (no. 51) and the *Catechism of the Catholic Church* (no. 1577). No one therefore, not even the supreme authority in the Church, can fail to accept this teaching without contradicting the will and example of Christ himself, and the economy of revelation which, as the dogmatic constitution *Dei Verbum* of the Second Vatican Council teaches, "is realized by deeds and words having an inner unity" (no. 2), in such a way that not only words but also deeds are sources of revelation and become words in the living memory of the Church.

Ordinatio Sacerdotalis notes however that, despite the constant and universal tradition of the Church and the teaching of the magisterium proposed anew in the above-mentioned recent documents, in some places the question continues to be considered as still open to debate or this teaching is held to be merely a matter of discipline. This widespread uncertainty explains and justifies the intervention of the magisterium of the supreme pontiff, explicitly in order "that all doubt may be removed regarding a matter of great importance" (no. 4) involving the correct understanding of Catholic teaching on the ministerial priesthood.

Certainly, the fact that the Church acknowledges that she does not have the authority to confer the ministerial priesthood on women also has repercussions on the discipline of the sacrament of orders. However, it is not for this reason merely a disciplinary matter. Rather, it is an expression of the truth according to which Jesus Christ conferred on the apostles and their successors the power of handing on the ministerial priesthood only to men. And given that the ministerial priesthood is one of the essential elements of the Church's structure, it follows that the question of who can receive priestly ordination "pertains to the Church's divine constitution itself" (no. 4).

The apostolic letter *Ordinatio Sacerdotalis*, in formally declaring the nature and the definitive force of this teaching, deriving from the will of Christ and the practice of the apostolic Church, confirms a certainty which has been constantly held and lived by the Church. It is not therefore a question of a new dogmatic formulation, but of a doctrine taught by the ordinary papal magisterium in a definitive way; that is, proposed not as a prudential teaching, nor as a more probable opinion nor as a mere matter of discipline, but as certainly true. Therefore, since it does not belong to matters freely open to dispute, it always requires the full and unconditional assent of the faithful, and to teach the contrary is equivalent to leading consciences into error. This declaration of the supreme pontiff is an act of listening to the word of God and of obedience to the Lord on the path of truth.

Pope John Paul II—also referring in this regard to the declaration *Inter Insigniores*—is likewise mindful of the need, felt particularly strongly today, to avoid in the Church all discrimination between men and women. In this regard the Holy Father recalls the figure of the Blessed Virgin Mary, mother of God and mother of the Church: The fact that she "received neither the mission proper to the apostles nor the ministerial priesthood clearly shows that the nonadmission of women to priestly ordination cannot mean that women are of lesser dignity nor can it be construed as discrimination against them" (no. 3). The ministerial priesthood depends on the economy of the mystery of Christ and the Church. Since it involves a sacrament, and not a form of social organization, the priesthood can be understood only in the light of Christ's revelation, handed down in scripture and interpreted by tradition. This does not imply any inferiority of women, whose presence and responsibility in the Church, though not linked to the ministerial priesthood, are absolutely necessary and irreplaceable, as is witnessed to in an exemplary way by the figure of the Virgin Mary.

Finally, as regards ecumenical dialogue, which is a dialogue in the truth, the apostolic letter *Ordinatio Sacerdotalis*, far from constituting an obstacle, can provide an opportunity for all Christians to deepen their understanding of the origin and theological nature of the episcopal and priestly ministry conferred by the sacrament of orders.

CONGREGATIO PRO DOCTRINA FIDEI

RESPONSUM AD DUBIUM CIRCA DOCTRINAM IN EPIST. AP. « ORDINATIO SACERDOTALIS » TRADITAM

Dub.: Utrum doctrina, tradita tamquam definitive tenenda in Epist. Ap. « Ordinatio Sacerdotalis », iuxta quam Ecclesia facultatem nullatenus habet ordinationem sacerdotalem mulieribus conferendi, ut pertinens *ad fidei depositum* intelligenda sit.

Resp.: Affirmative.

Haec enim doctrina assensum definitivum exigit, cum, in verbo Dei scripto fundata atque in Ecclesiae Traditione inde ab initio constanter servata et applicata, ab ordinario et universali magisterio infallibiliter proposita sit (cf Conc. Vat. II, const. dogm. *Lumen Gentium,* 25,2). Quapropter, praesentibus adiunctis, Romanus Pontifex, proprium munus fratres confirmandi exercens (cf *Lc* 22,32), eandem doctrinam per formalem declarationem tradidit, explicite enuntians quod semper, quod ubique et quod ab omnibus tenendum est, utpote ad fidei depositum pertinens.

Hoc responsum in Conventu ordinario huius Congregationis deliberatum, Summus Pontifex Ioannes Paulus PP. II, in Audientia infrascripto Cardinali Praefecto concessa, adprobavit et publici iuris fieri iussit.

Romae, ex aedibus Congregationis pro Doctrina Fidei, die 28 mensis octobris 1995, in festo SS. Simonis et Iudae, Apostolorum.

✠ Josephus Card. Ratzinger
Praefectus

✠ Tarcisius Bertone
Archiep. emeritus Vercellen.
Secretarius

CONGREGATION FOR THE DOCTRINE OF THE FAITH

REPLY TO THE "DUBIUM" CONCERNING THE DOCTRINE CONTAINED IN THE APOSTOLIC LETTER "ORDINATIO SACERDOTALIS"

Dubium: Whether the teaching that the Church has no authority whatsoever to confer priestly ordination on women, which is presented in the apostolic letter *Ordinatio Sacerdotalis* to be held definitively, is to be understood as belonging to the deposit of the faith.

Responsum: In the affirmative.

This teaching requires definitive assent, since, founded on the written word of God and from the beginning constantly preserved and applied in the tradition of the Church, it has been set forth infallibly by the ordinary and universal magisterium (cf. Second Vatican Council, Dogmatic Constitution on the Church *Lumen Gentium,* 25, 2). Thus, in the present circumstances, the Roman pontiff, exercising his proper office of confirming the brethren (cf. Lk 22:32), has handed on this same teaching by a formal declaration, explicitly stating what is to be held always, everywhere, and by all, as belonging to the deposit of the faith.

The Sovereign Pontiff John Paul II, at the audience granted to the undersigned Cardinal Prefect, approved this reply, adopted in the ordinary session of this congregation, and ordered it to be published.

Rome, from the Offices of the Congregation for the Doctrine of the Faith on the Feast of the Apostles SS. Simon and Jude, October 28, 1995.

✠ Joseph Card. Ratzinger
Prefect

✠ Tarcisio Bertone
Archbishop Emeritus of Vercelli
Secretary

CONCERNING THE REPLY OF THE CONGREGATION FOR THE DOCTRINE OF THE FAITH ON THE DOCTRINE CONTAINED IN THE APOSTOLIC LETTER "ORDINATIO SACERDOTALIS"

The publication of the Reply of the Congregation for the Doctrine of the Faith to a *dubium* regarding the reason for which the teaching contained in the apostolic letter *Ordinatio Sacerdotalis* is to be considered *definitive tenenda* seems the appropriate moment to offer certain reflections.

The ecclesiological significance of this apostolic letter was underscored even by its date of publication, for it was on that day, 22 May 1994, that the Church celebrated the Solemnity of Pentecost. Its importance, however, could be discovered above all in the concluding words of the letter: "in order that all doubt may be removed regarding a matter of great importance, a matter which pertains to the Church's divine constitution itself, in virtue of my ministry of confirming the brethren (cf. Lk 22:32), I declare that the Church has no authority whatsoever to confer priestly ordination on women and that this judgment is to be definitively held by all the Church's faithful" (no. 4).

The pope's intervention was necessary not simply to reiterate the validity of a discipline observed in the Church from the beginning, but to confirm a doctrine "preserved by the constant and universal tradition of the Church and firmly taught by the magisterium in its more recent documents," which "pertains to the Church's divine constitution itself" (no. 4). In this way, the Holy Father intended to make clear that the teaching that priestly ordination is to be reserved solely to men could not be considered "open to debate" and neither could one attribute to the decision of the Church "a merely disciplinary force" (ibid.).

The fruits of this letter have been evident since its publication. Many consciences which in good faith had been disturbed, more by doubt than by uncertainty, found serenity once again thanks to the teaching of the Holy Father. However, some perplexity continued, not only among those who, distant from the Catholic faith, do not accept the existence of a doctrinal authority within the Church—that is, a magisterium sacramentally invested with the authority of Christ (cf. *Lumen Gentium,* no. 21)—but also among some of the faithful to whom it continued to seem that the exclusion of women from the priestly ministry represents a form of injustice or discrimination against them. Some objected that it is not evident from revelation that such an exclusion was the will of Christ for his Church, and others had questions concerning the assent owed to the letter.

Certainly, the understanding of the reasons for which the Church does not have the power to confer priestly ordination on women can be deepened further. Such reasons, for example, have been set out already in the declaration *Inter Insigniores* (15 October 1976), issued by the Congregation for the Doctrine of the Faith and approved by Pope Paul VI, and in a number of the documents of John Paul II (for example, *Christifidelis Laici,* no. 51; *Mulieris Dignitatem,* no. 26; as well as in the *Catechism of the Catholic Church,* no. 1577). But in any case it cannot be forgotten that the Church teaches, as an absolutely fundamental truth of Christian anthropology, the equal personal dignity of men and women, and the necessity of overcoming and doing away with "every type of discrimination regarding fundamental rights" *(Gaudium et Spes,* no. 29). It is in the light of this truth that one can seek to understand better the teaching that women cannot receive priestly ordination. A correct theology can prescind neither from one nor from the other of these doctrines, but most hold the two together; only thus will it be able to deepen our comprehension of God's plan regarding woman and regarding the priesthood—and hence, regarding the mission of woman in the Church. If, however, perhaps by allowing oneself to be conditioned too much by the ways and spirit of the age, one should assert that a contradiction exists between these two truths, the way of progress in the intelligence of the faith would be lost.

In the letter *Ordinatio Sacerdotalis* the pope focuses attention on the figure of the blessed Virgin Mary, Mother of God, and Mother of the Church. The fact that she "received neither the mission proper to the apostles nor the ministerial priesthood clearly shows that the non-admission of women to priestly ordination cannot mean that women are of lesser dignity, nor can it be construed as discrimination against them" (no. 3). Diversity of mission in no way compromises equality of personal dignity.

Furthermore, to understand that this teaching implies no injustice or discrimination against women, one has to consider the nature of the ministerial priesthood itself, which is a service and not a position of privilege or human power over others. Whoever, man or woman, conceives of the priesthood in terms of personal affirmation, as a goal or point of departure in a career of human success, is profoundly mistaken, for the true meaning of Christian priesthood, whether it be the common priesthood of the faithful or, in a most special way, the ministerial priesthood, can only be found in the sacrifice of one's own being in union with Christ, in service of the brethren. Priestly ministry constitutes neither the universal ideal nor, even less, the goal of Christian life. In this connection, it is helpful to recall once again that "the only higher gift, which can and must be desired, is charity" (cf. 1 Cor 12:13; *Inter Insigniores*, VI).

With respect to its foundation in Sacred Scripture and in tradition, John Paul II directs his attention to the fact that the Lord Jesus, as is witnessed by the New Testament, called only men, and not women, to the ordained ministry, and that the apostles "did the same when they chose fellow workers who would succeed them in their ministry" (no. 2; cf. 1 Tm 3:1ff; 2 Tm 1:6; Ti 1:5). There are sound arguments supporting the fact that Christ's way of acting was not determined by cultural motives (cf. no. 2), as there are also sufficient grounds to state that tradition has interpreted the choice made by the Lord as binding for the Church of all times.

Here, however, we find ourselves before the essential interdependence of Holy Scripture and tradition, an interdependence which makes of these two forms of the transmission of the Gospel an unbreakable unity with the magisterium, which is an integral part of tradition and is entrusted with the authentic interpretation of the word of God, written and handed down *(Dei Verbum,* nos. 9 and 10). In the specific case of priestly ordination, the successors of the apostles have always observed the norm of conferring it only on men, and the magisterium, assisted by the Holy Spirit, teaches us that this did not occur by chance, habitual repetition, subjection to sociological conditioning, or even less because of some imaginary inferiority of women; but rather because "the Church has always acknowledged as a perennial norm her Lord's way of acting in choosing the twelve men whom he made the foundation of his Church" (no. 2).

As is well known, there are reasons *ex convenienta* by which theology has sought and seeks to understand the reasonableness of the will of the Lord. Such reasons, expounded for example in the declaration *Inter Insigniores,* have their undoubted values, and yet they are not conceived or employed as if they were strictly logical proofs derived from absolute principles. At the same time, it is important to keep in mind, as these reasons help us to comprehend, that the human will of Christ not only is not arbitrary, but that it is intimately united with the divine will of the eternal Son, on which the ontological and anthropological truth of the creation of the two sexes depends.

In response to this precise act of the magisterium of the Roman pontiff, explicitly addressed to the entire Catholic Church, all members of the faithful are required to give their assent to the teaching stated therein. To this end, the Congregation for the Doctrine of the Faith, with the approval of the Holy Father, has given an official reply on the nature of this assent: it is a matter of full definitive assent, that is to say, irrevocable, to a doctrine taught infallibly by the Church. In fact, as the reply explains, the definitive nature of this assent derives from the truth of the doctrine itself, since, founded on the written word of God, and constantly held and applied in the tradition of the Church, it has been set forth infallibly by the ordinary universal magisterium (cf. *Lumen Gentium,* no. 25). Thus, the reply specifies that this doctrine belongs to the deposit of the faith of the Church. It should be emphasized that the definitive and infallible nature of this teaching of the Church did not arise with the publication of the letter *Ordinatio Sacerdotalis*. In the letter, as the reply of the Congregation for the Doctrine of the Faith also explains, the Roman pontiff, having taken account of present circumstances, has confirmed the same teaching by a formal declaration, giving expression once again to *quod semper, quod ubique et quod ab omnibus tenendum est, utpote ad fidei depositum pertinens*. In this case, an act of the ordinary papal magisterium, in itself not infallible, witnesses to the infallibility of the teaching of a doctrine already possessed by the Church.

Finally, there have been some commentaries on the letter *Ordinatio Sacerdotalis* which have suggested that the document constitutes an additional and inopportune obstacle on the already difficult path of ecumenism. In this regard, it should not be forgotten that according to both the letter and the spirit of the Second Vatican Council (cf. *Unitatis Redintegratio*, no. 11), the authentic ecumenical task, to which the Catholic Church is unequivocally and permanently committed, requires complete sincerity and clarity in the presentation of one's own faith. Furthermore, it should be noted that the doctrine reaffirmed by the letter *Ordinatio Sacerdotalis* cannot but further the pursuit of full communion with the Orthodox Churches which, in fidelity to tradition, have maintained and continue to maintain the same teaching.

The singular originality of the Church and of the priestly ministry within the Church requires a precise clarity of criteria. Concretely, one must never lose sight of the fact that the Church does not find the source of her faith and her constitutive structure in the principles of the social order of any historical period. While attentive to the world in which she lives and for whose salvation she labors, the Church is conscious of being the bearer of a higher fidelity to which she is bound. It is a question of a radical faithfulness to the word of God which she has received from Christ who established her to last until the end of the ages. This word of God, in proclaiming the essential value and eternal destiny of each person, reveals the ultimate foundation of the dignity of every being, of every woman, and of every man.

SOURCES

Declaration "Inter Insigniores"

Latin text: *AAS*, LXIX (1971)
English text: *Origins* 33:6 (1977): 517-524

Congregation for the Doctrine of the Faith. "A Commentary on the Declaration." *Origins* 33:6 (1977): 524-531.

RAIMONDO SPIAZZI, OP. "The Advancement of Women According to the Church." *L'Osservatore Romano* (February 10, 1977): 6-7.

ALBERT DESCAMPS. "Significance for Us Today of Christ's Attitude and of the Practice of the Apostles." *L'Osservatore Romano* (February 17, 1977): 6-7.

HANS URS VON BALTHASAR. "The Uninterrupted Tradition of the Church." *L'Osservatore Romano* (February 24, 1977): 6-7.

A. G. MARTIMORT. "The Value of a Theological Formula '*In Persona Christi.*'" *L'Osservatore Romano* (March 10, 1977): 6-7.

GUSTAVE MARTELET, SJ. "The Mystery of the Covenant and Its Connections with the Nature of the Ministerial Priesthood." *L'Osservatore Romano* (March 17, 1977): 6-7.

JOSEPH L. BERNARDIN. "The Ministerial Priesthood and the Advancement of Women." *L'Osservatore Romano* (March 3, 1977): 3-4.

JOSEPH RATZINGER. "The Male Priesthood: A Violation of Women's Rights?" *L'Osservatore Romano* (May 12, 1977): 6-7.

ALBERT VANHOYE, SJ. "Church's Practice in Continuity with New Testament Teaching." *L'Osservatore Romano* 10:10 (March 1993): 10-11.

INOS BIFFI. "Church's Stance Continues the Practice of Christ and the Apostles." *L'Osservatore Romano* 11:17 (March 1993): 8.

MAX THURIAN. "Marian Profile of Ministry Is Basis of Woman's Ecclesial Role." *L'Osservatore Romano* 24:12 (March 1993): 8.

JEAN CORBON. "Ordination of Women Creates Serious Ecumenical Problems." *L'Osservatore Romano* 31:13 (March 1993): 10.

JUTTA BURGGRAF. "Woman's Spiritual Motherhood Attests to God's Mercy and Love." *L'Osservatore Romano* 7:14 (April 1993): 10.

JOYCE LITTLE. "Women Are Called to Bear Christ into Their Families and the World." *L'Osservatore Romano* 24:15 (April 1993): 6.

Apostolic Letter "Ordinatio Sacerdotalis"

Latin text: AAS, LXXXVX (1994): 545-548
English text: Origins 24:4 (June 9, 1994): 49-52

"Reply to the 'Dubium' Concerning the Teaching Contained in the Apostolic Letter *Ordinatio Sacerdotalis*." *L'Osservatore Romano* 22:47 (November 1995): 2.

"Concerning the Reply of the Congregation for the Doctrine of the Faith on the Teaching Contained in the Apostolic Letter *Ordinatio Sacerdotalis*." *L'Osservatore Romano* 22:47 (November 1995): 2-3.